Aurélien Froment
Pulmo Marina

Photographed and filmed
at the Monterey Bay Aquarium,
California, 19 February 2010
Production: Franck Isabel,
La bise au chat, Paris
Production assistant: Eve Portal
Cameraman: Ernie Kovács
Camera assistant: Philip Powell
Camera: HDCAM F900
Digitizing: Todd Lindo,
Roughhouse, San Francisco
Color grading: Richard Etchells,
Technicolor, London

Text: Aurélien Froment
Translated from the French
by Deke Dusinberre

Originally commissioned as a film
by the Independent Cinema Office
and LUX with support from the
National Lottery through Arts
Council England

Thanks to Jenny Slafkosky
and Chad L. Widmer at the
Monterey Bay Aquarium

First published in
Great Britain in 2011
by Dent-De-Leone
48 Wilton Way
E8 1BG London, Uk
www.dentedeleone.co.nz
info@dentdeleone.co.nz

ISBN 978-1-907908-00-2

Texts, Images © the
author, all rights reserved
in accordance with the
provisions of the copyright
designs and patents act, 1988

This book was made possible
by way of subscription
through the generous
patience and trust of its
readers, with support from
Kadist Art Foundation, Motive
Gallery and Drac Ile-de-France.
(bourse individuelle à la
création, 2008).

Designed by åbäke
Printed by Die Keure, Belgium
This publication is set
in Marionette.
Printed in 1000 copies

In Alphabetical Order

————————————————

Pulmo Marina

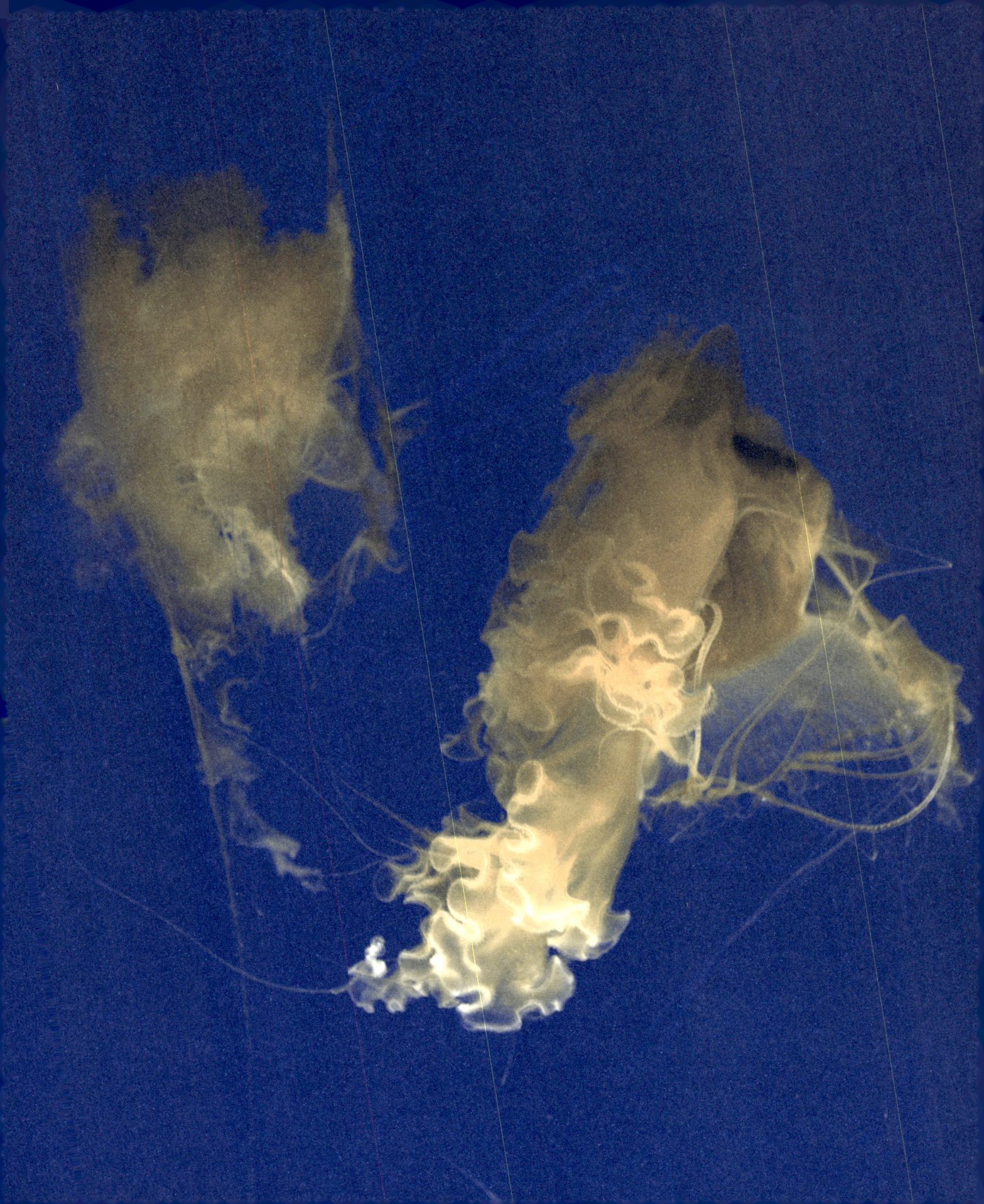

Pulmo Marina

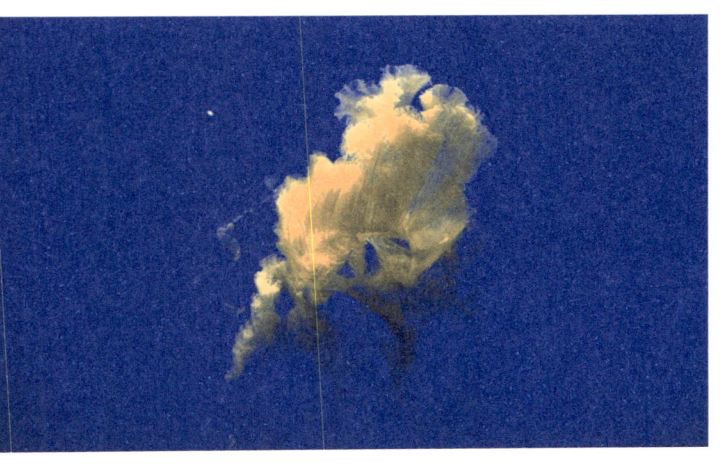

A mouth that
looks like a root

A gelatinous bag
edged with filaments

Stamens and a pistil

A sea lung

Remember the Flying
Toasters? 1940-style
chrome toasters sporting
bird-like wings, flying
across the darkness with
pieces of brown toast?

I can see that
grin on your face.

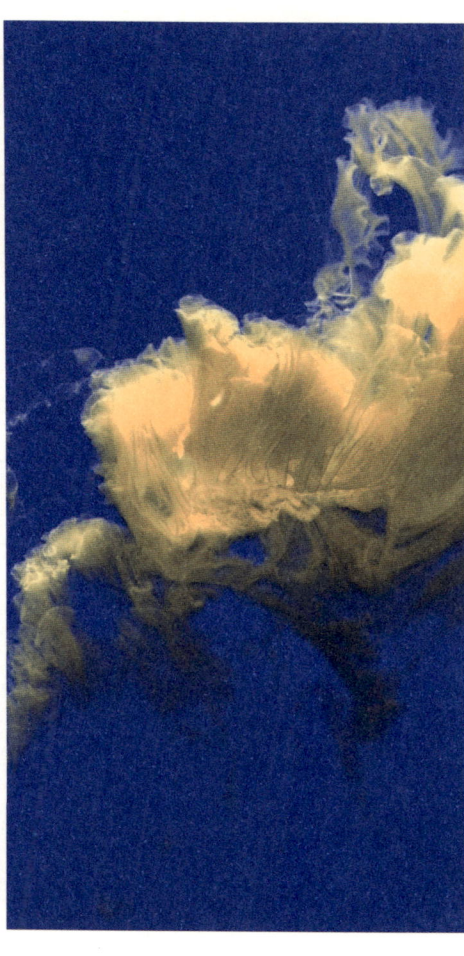

Two currents swirl, from bottom to top, opposite one another, leaving a neutral space in the middle where the drifter is held in a stationary position.

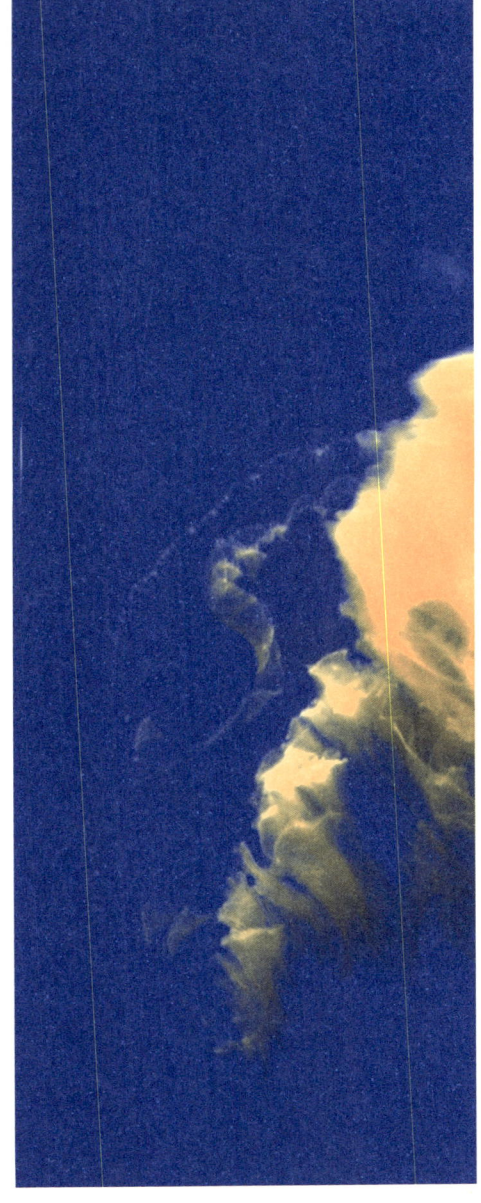

Its name, Kreisel, comes from the spinning tops that kids used to play with, which refers here to the circulation of water inside the tank.

Every night, seawater from the bay is pumped into the tank, supplying the animals with plankton and other copepods.

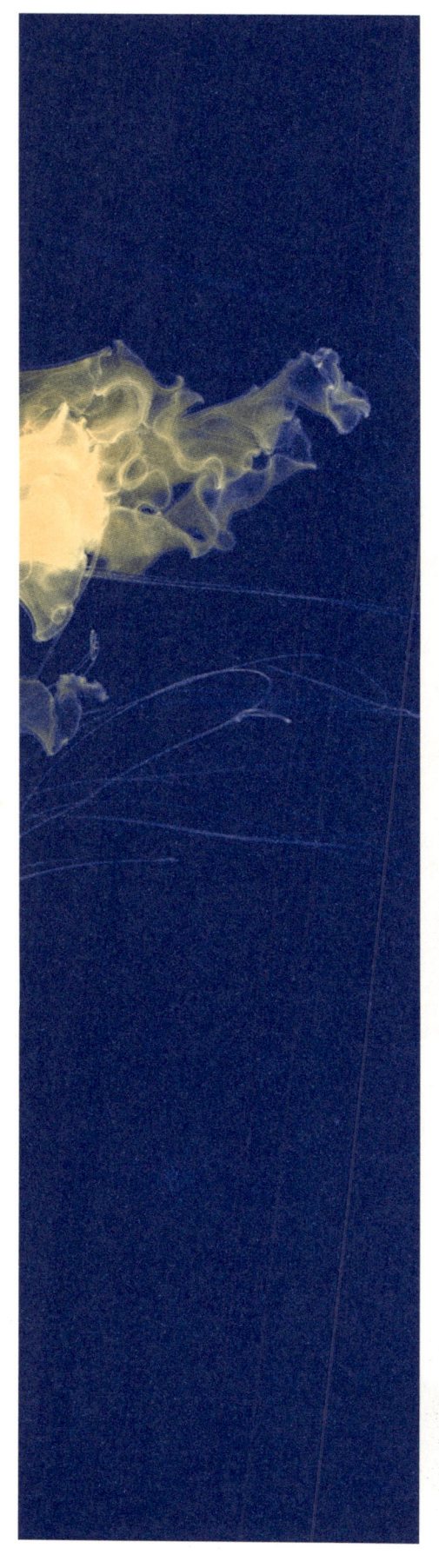

Some tanks are round, but this one is elliptical. It was based on a German design developed in the 1960s.

The strong colour-contrast
between blue and yellow
was created by two
spotlights placed off-
screen, on opposite sides
of the tank.

The blue background is
created by an opaque sheet
of colored acrylic.

A neon tube placed behind
it casts light in a fairly
even way.

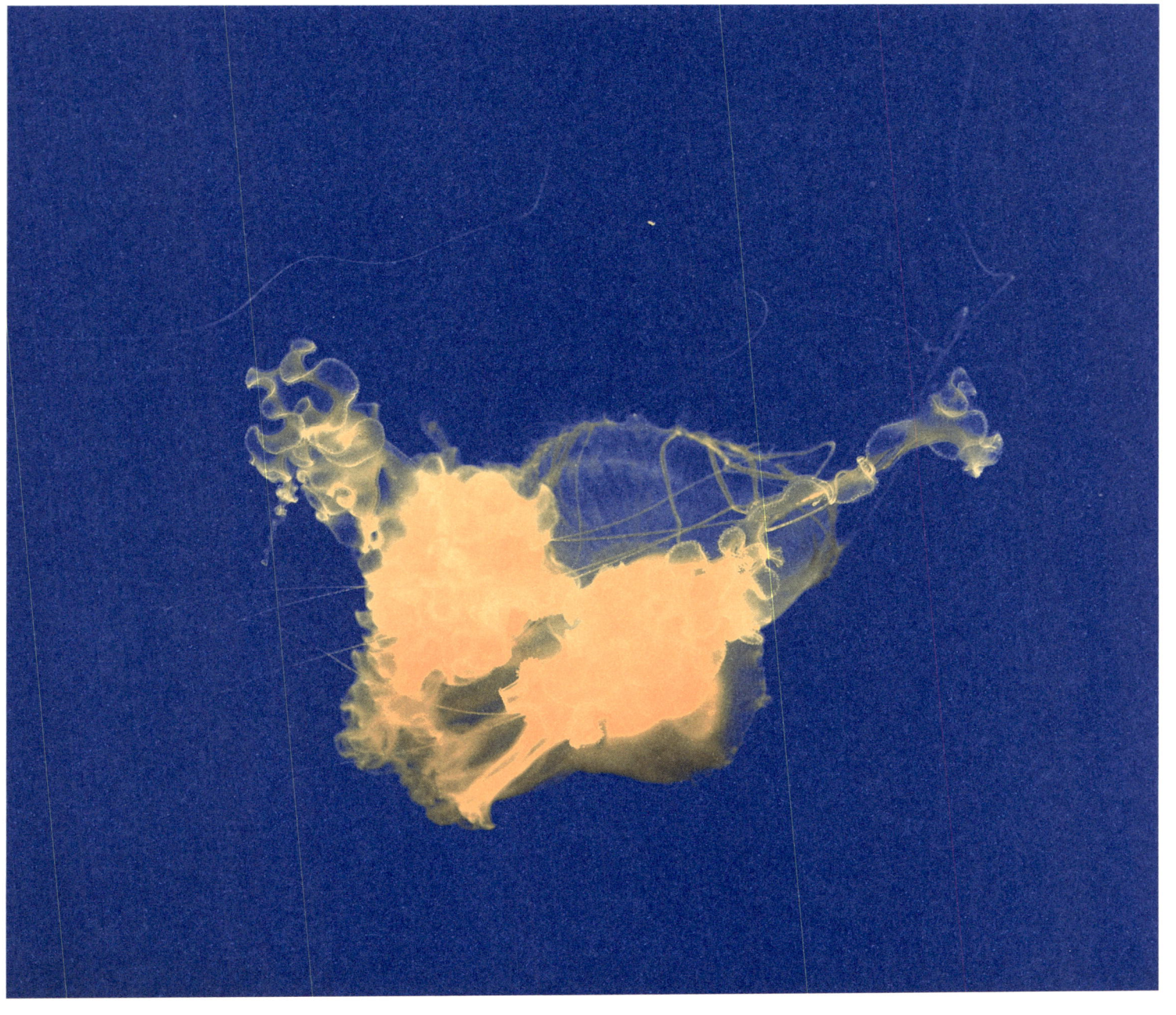

The transparent sheet of acrylic that we're looking through is two inches thick. It is set into a window five feet wide and three feet high. Although you couldn't dip much more than your forearm into it, the tank looks infinite, like the landscapes behind the windows of the dioramas at the American Museum of Natural History in New York.

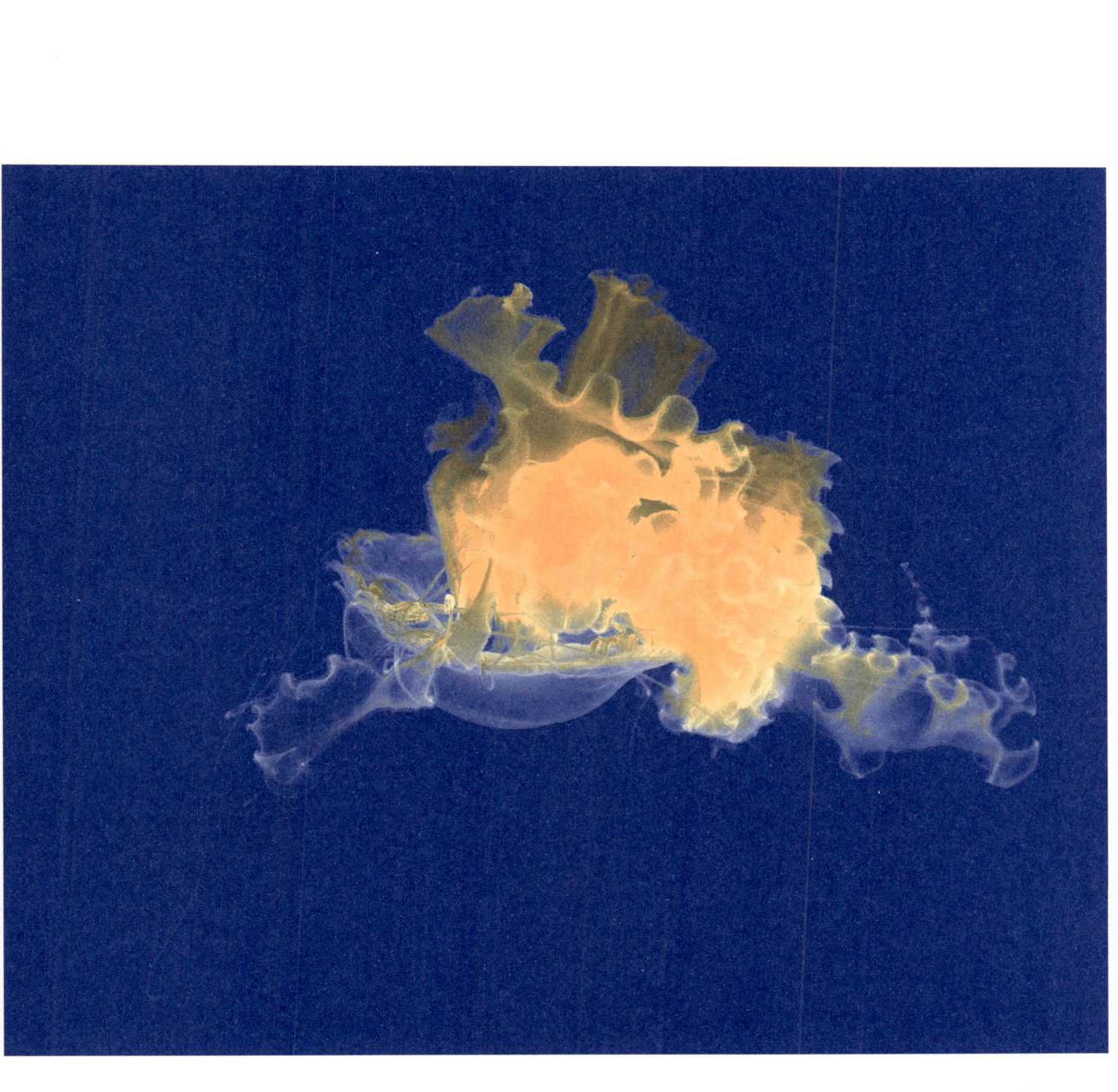

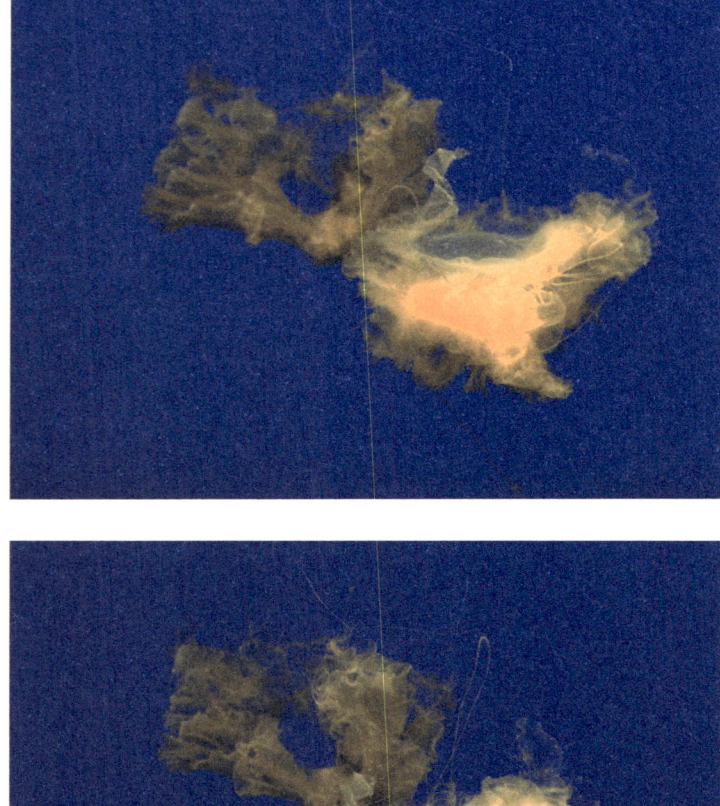

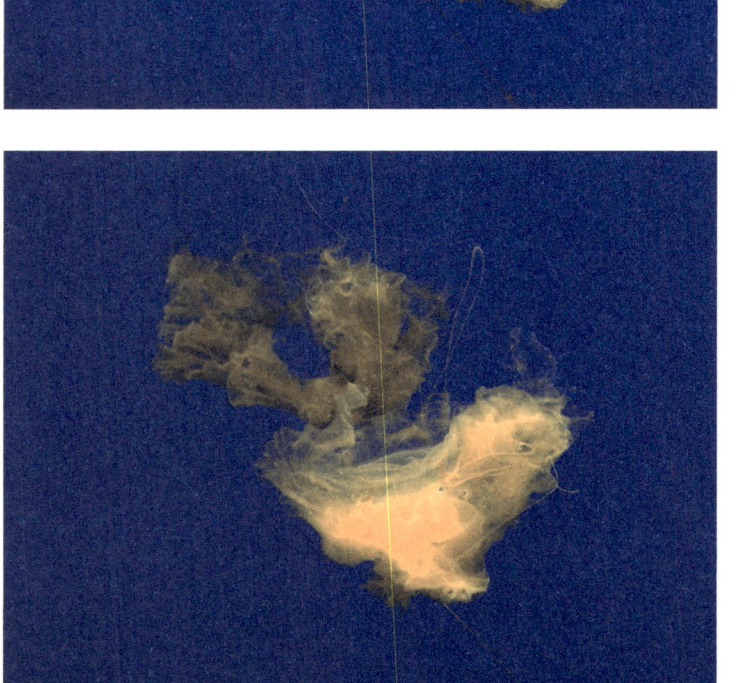

A large, rectangular, electric-blue window lights the way.

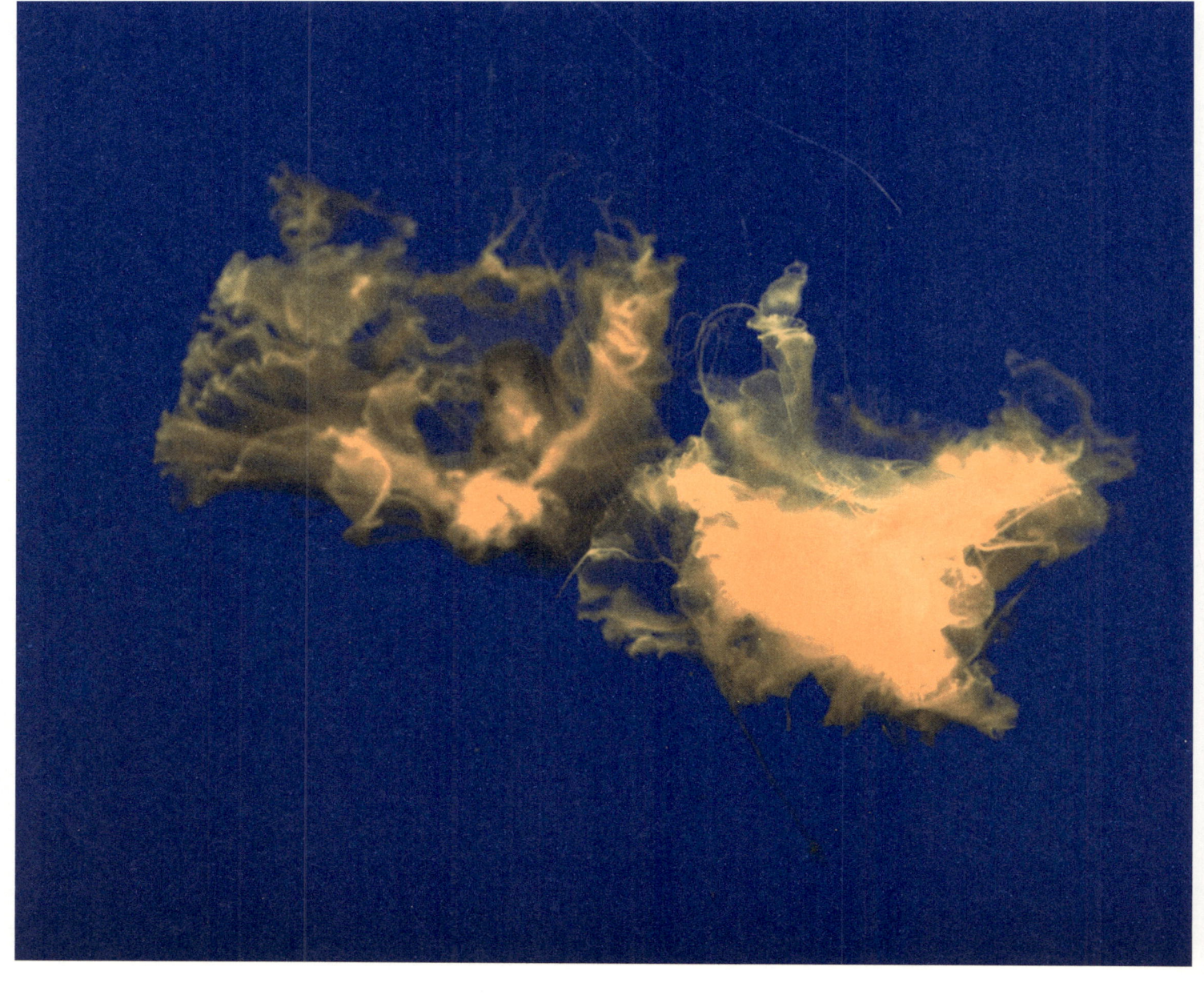

The room is totally dark.

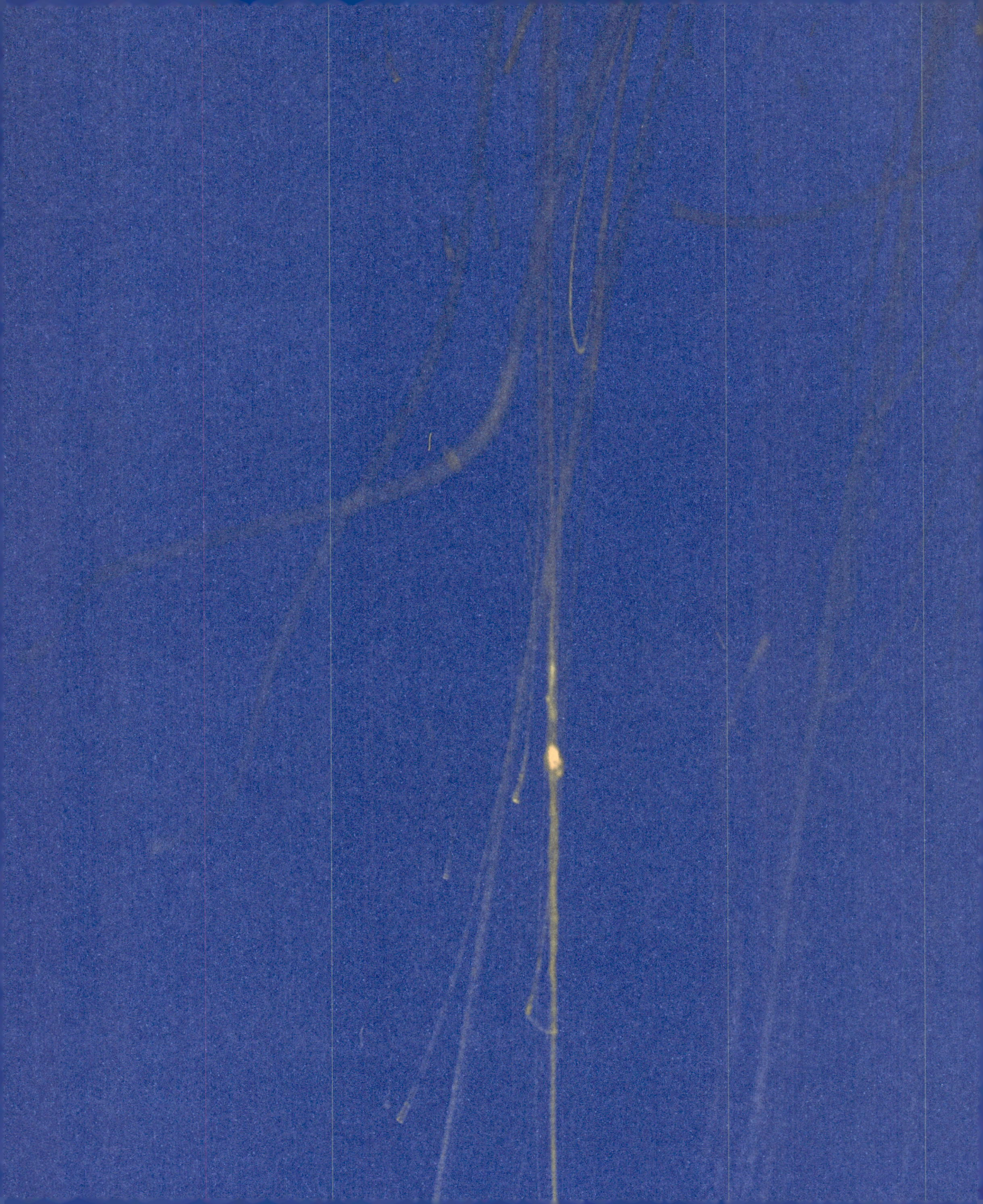

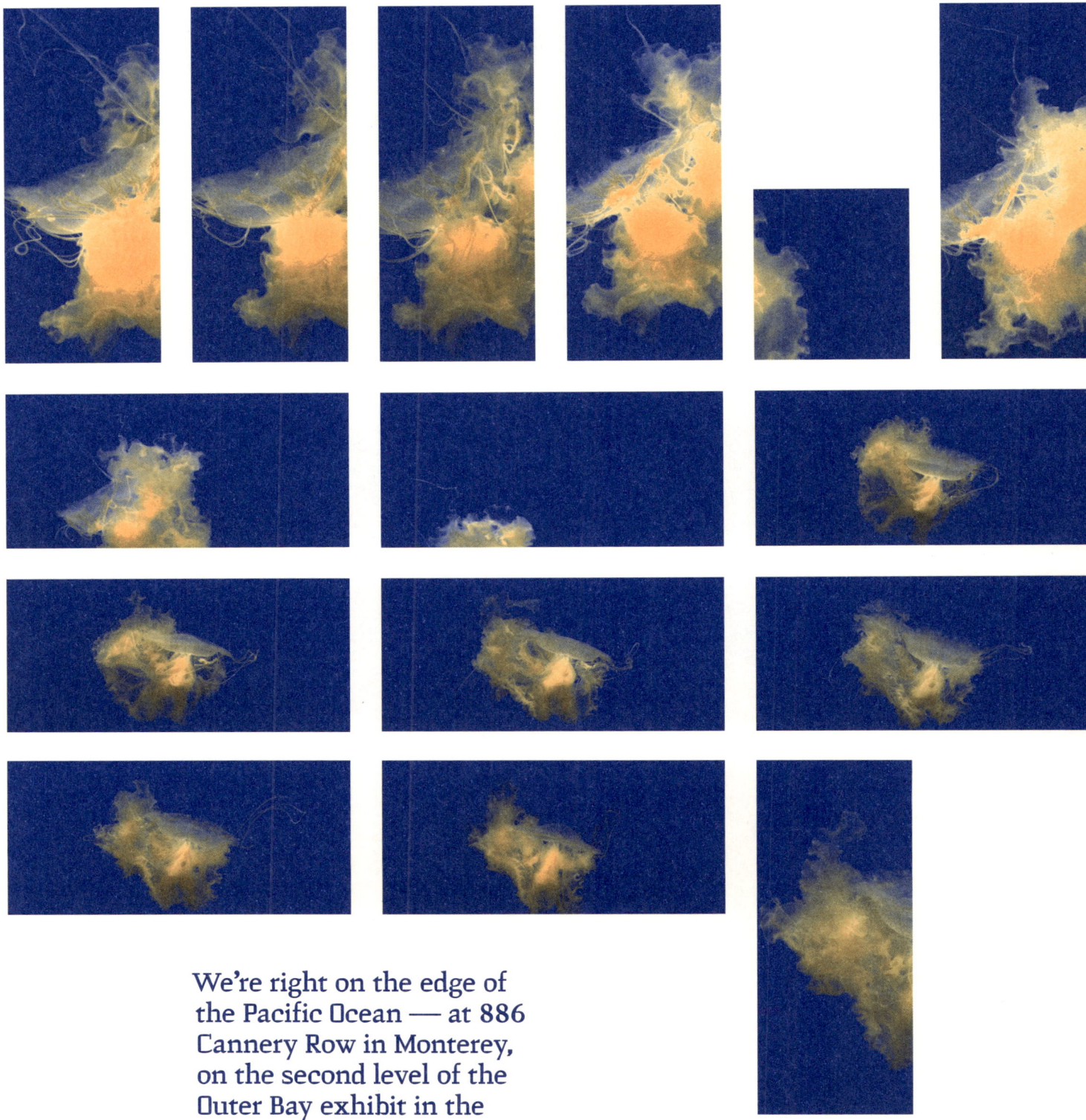

We're right on the edge of the Pacific Ocean — at 886 Cannery Row in Monterey, on the second level of the Outer Bay exhibit in the Monterey Bay Aquarium.

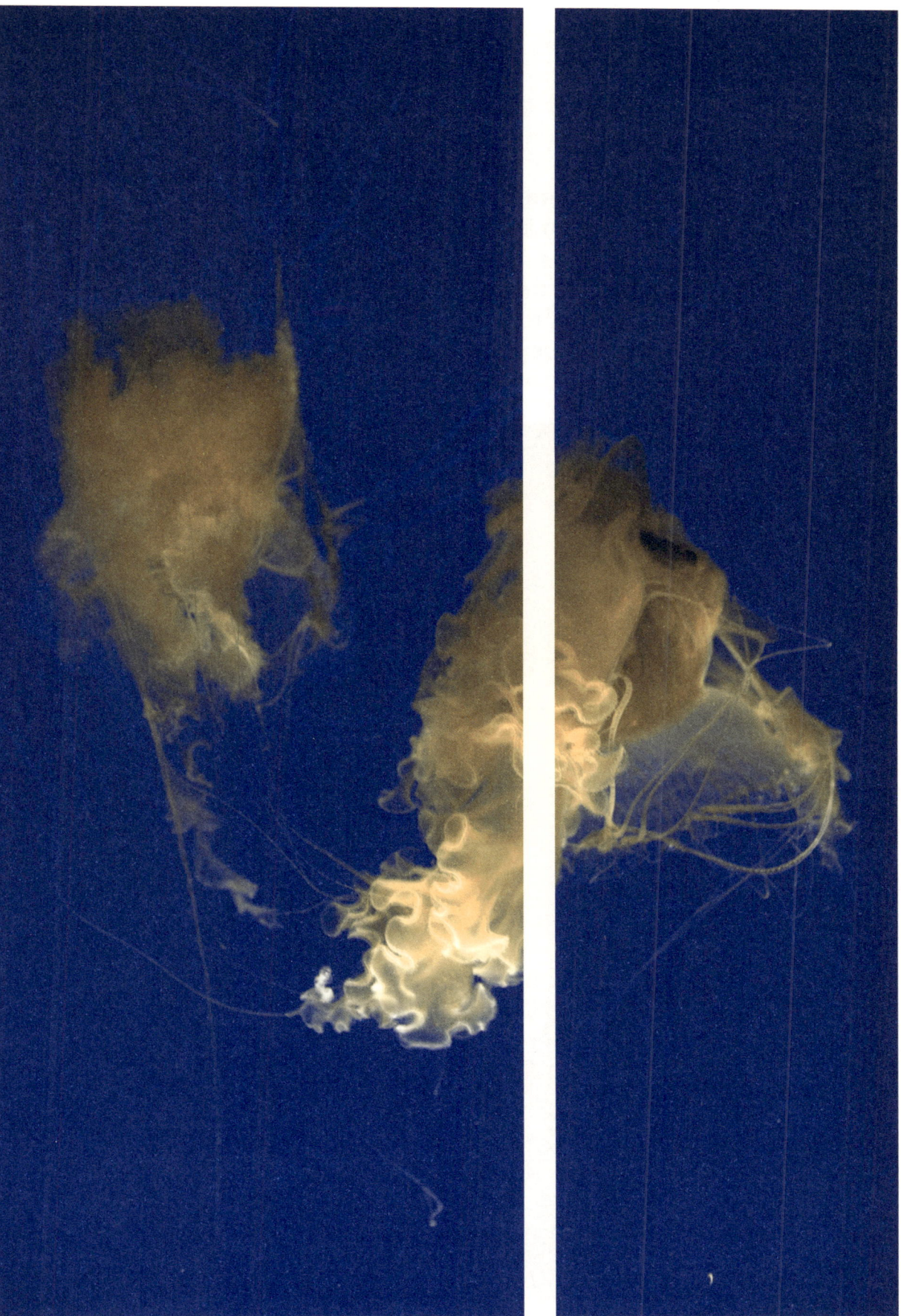

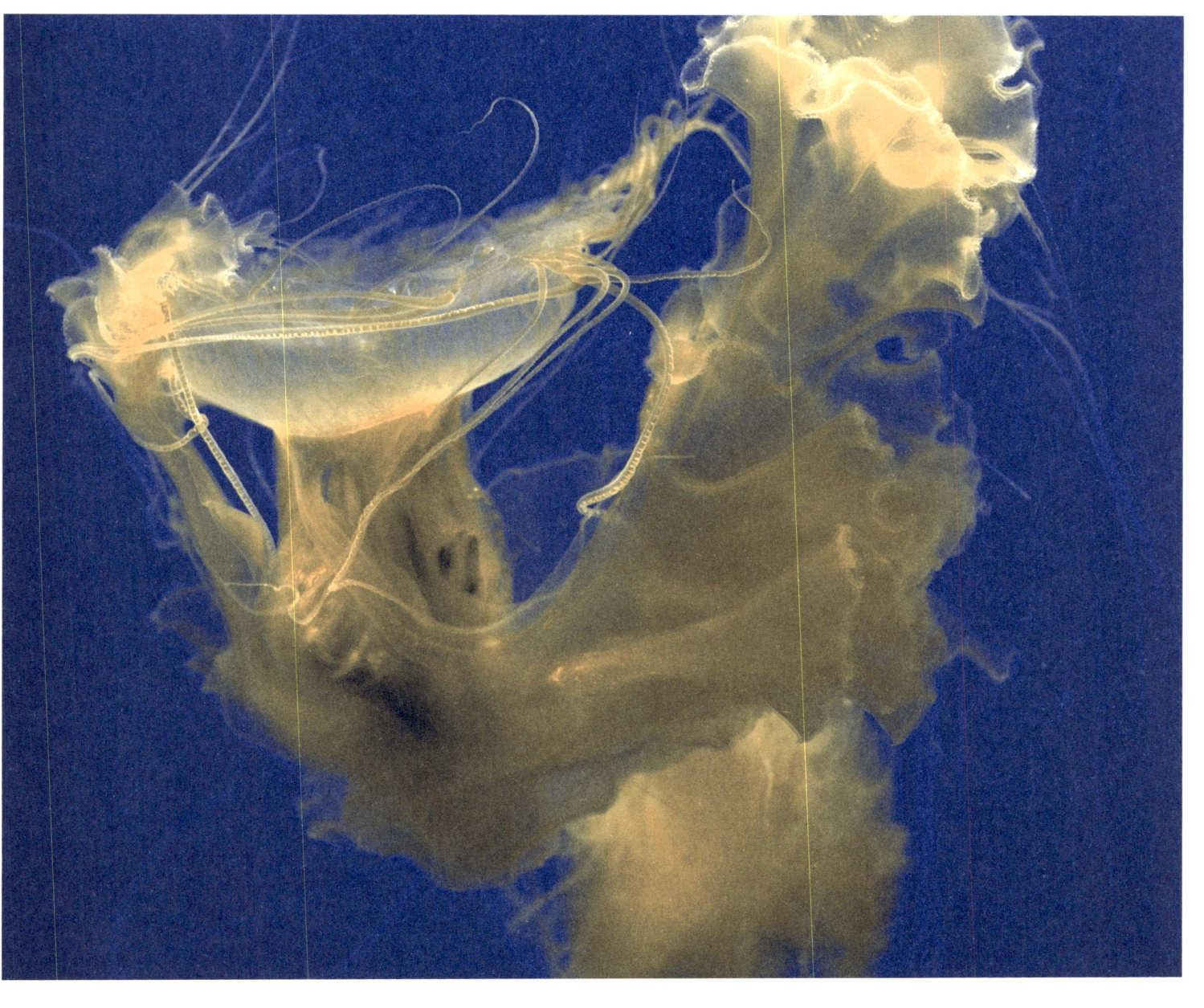

Their lifecycle hasn't been
completely documented yet.
If you stuck a tag on them to
track them, the way certain fish
are tagged these days, they
would sink instantly.

So all that we know about
them is what we can observe
in a lab aquarium.

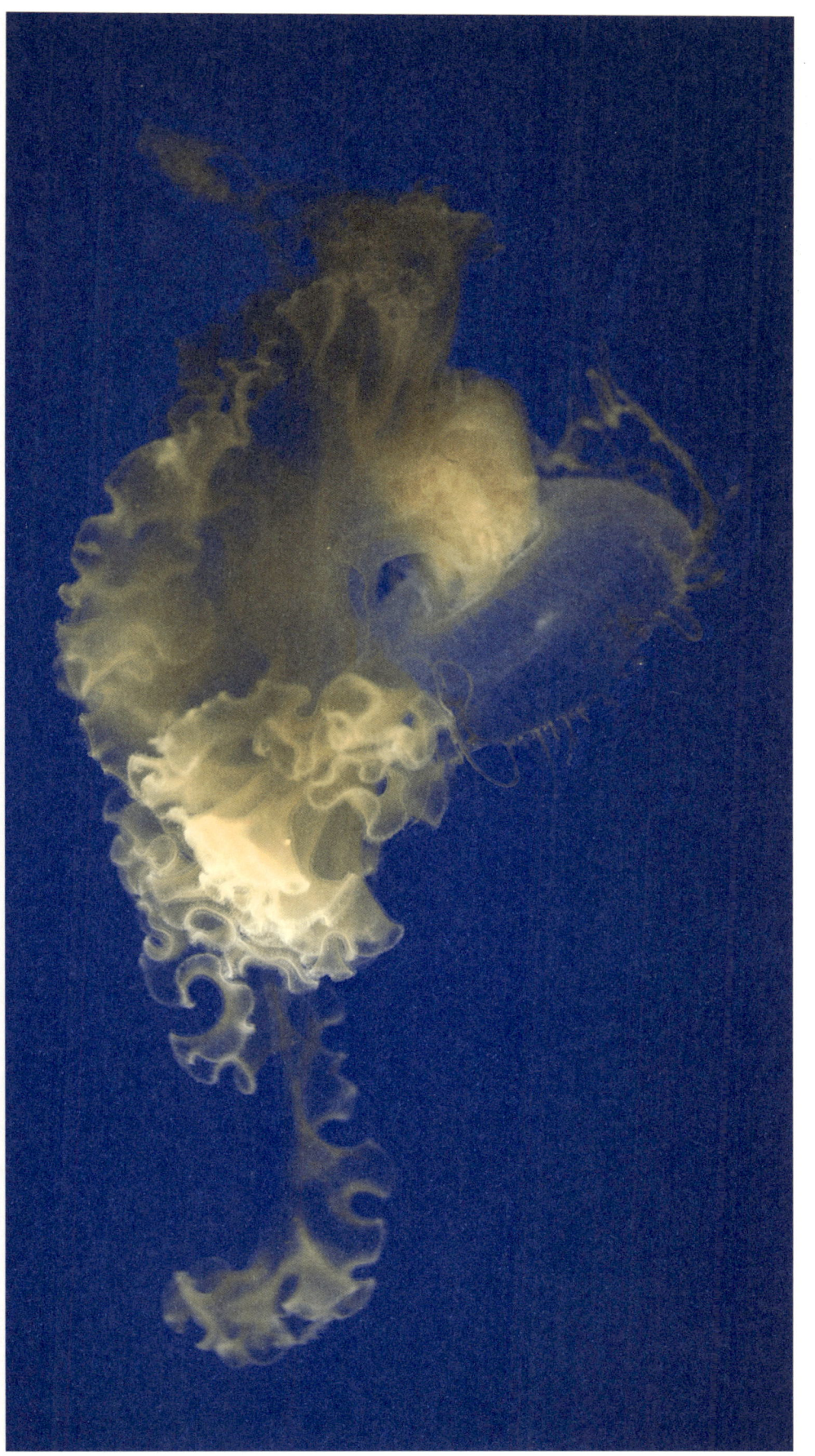

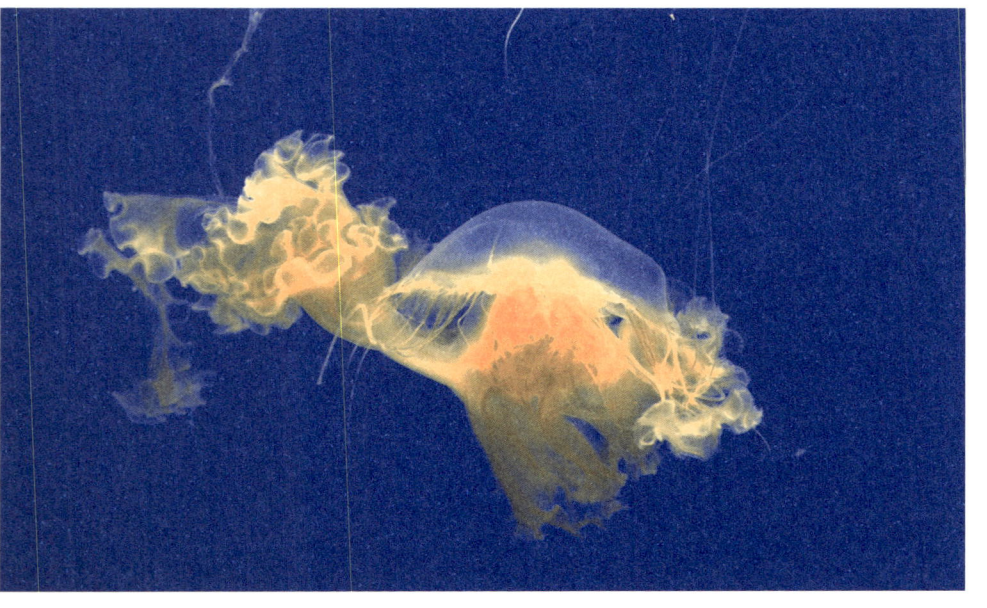

The unfortunate victims
are paralyzed by cnidocytes
scattered in the epidermis
of the tentacles and
sometimes on the bell,
where they gather in
little warts.

Then the victims are
swallowed by the mouth
and dispatched to the
stomach.

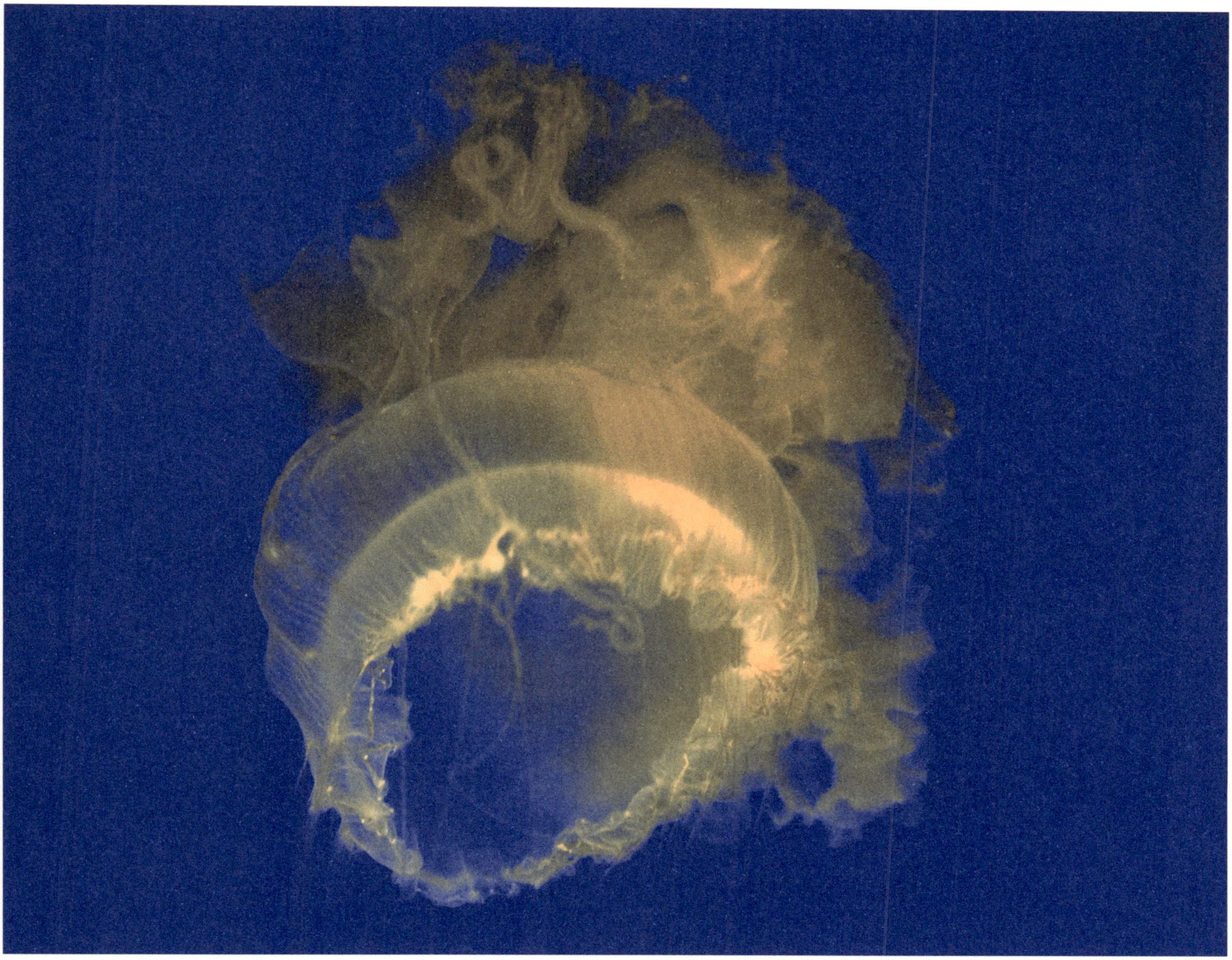

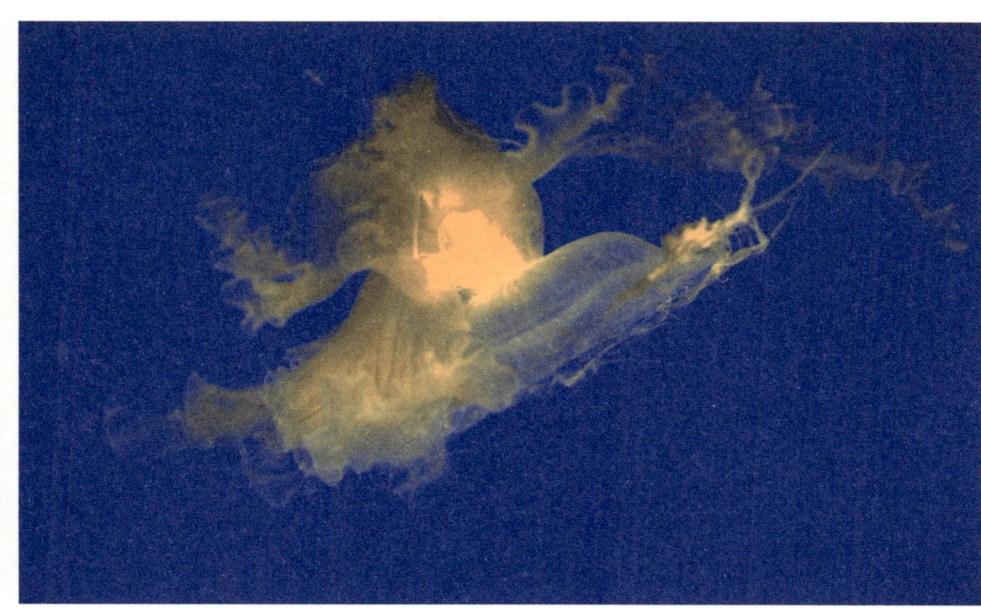

At the top of the food chain,
the Egg-Yolk jelly can eat
all the others: Crystal
Jelly, Moon Jelly, Polyorchis
Haplus or Pacific Sea Nettle.

Jellyfish are intrepid
carnivores— they eat
other jellyfish.

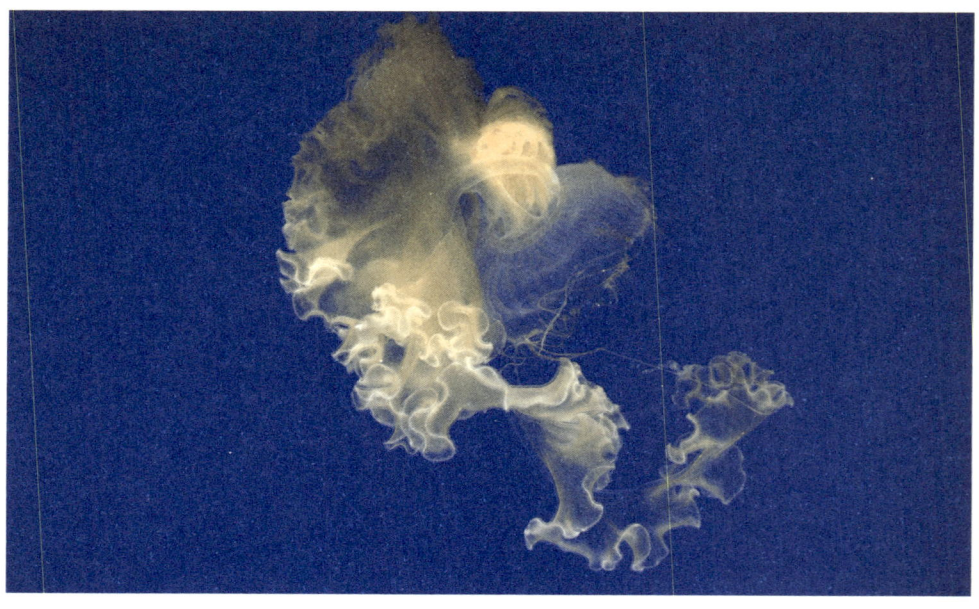

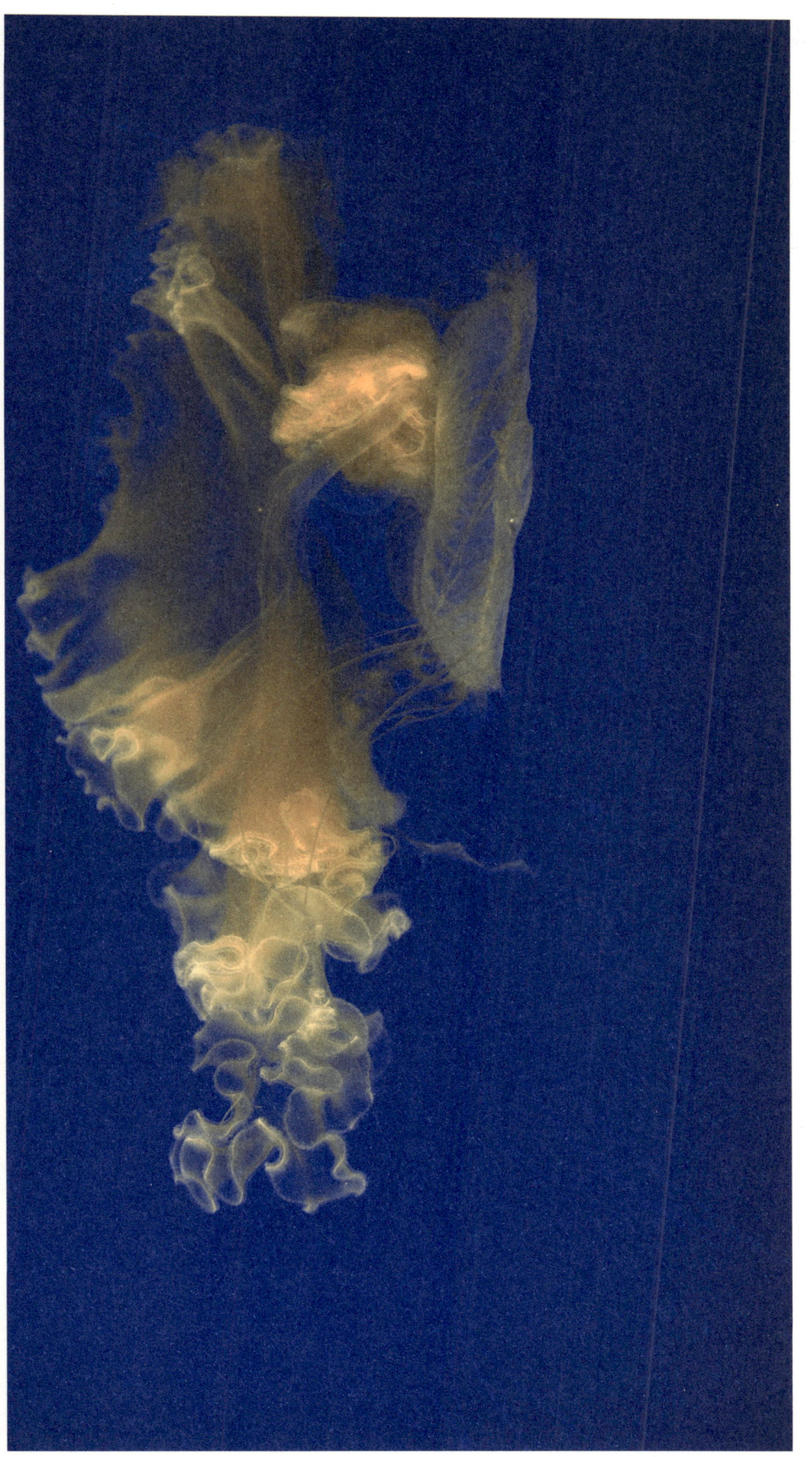

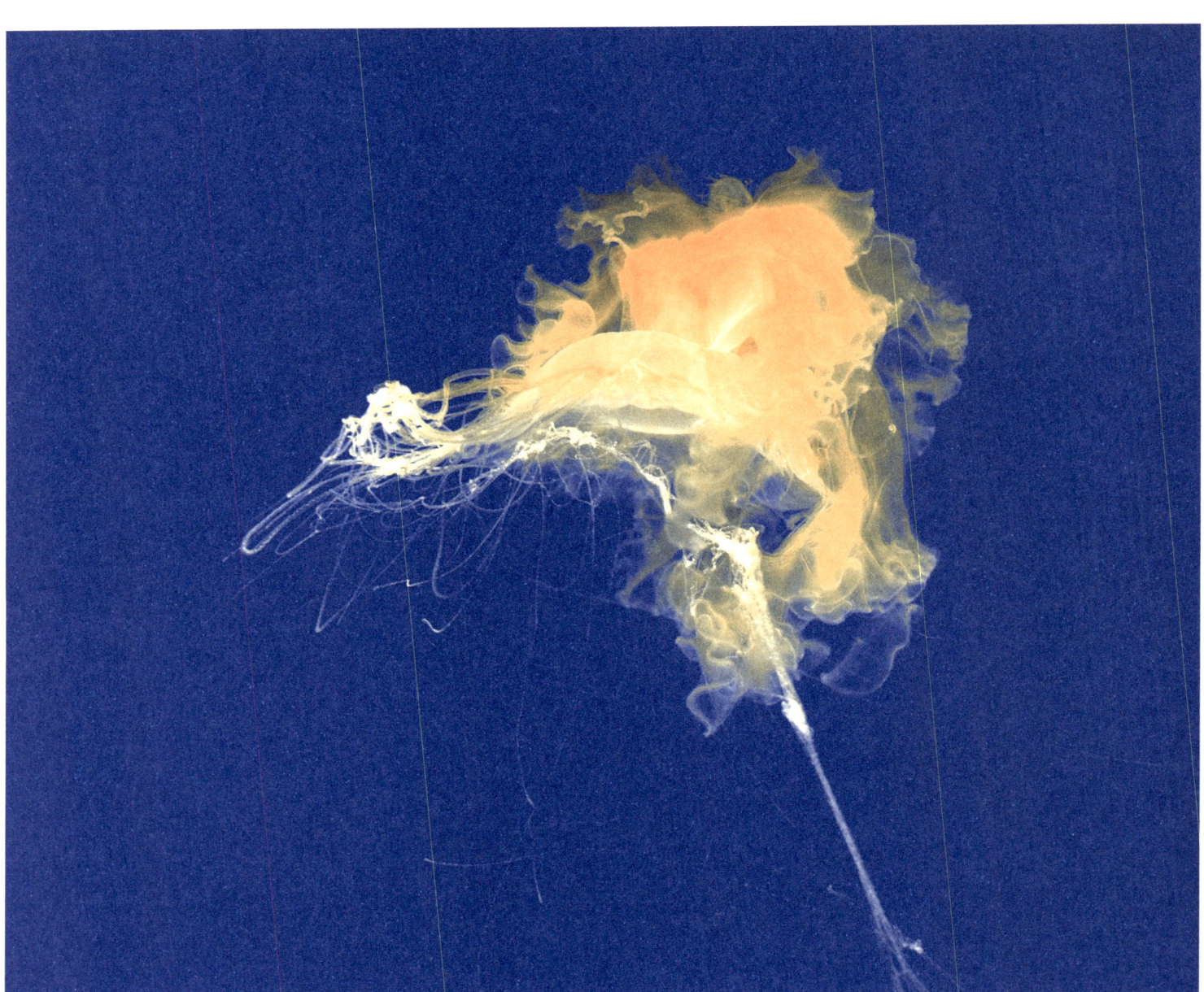

With their serpent-like tentacles and stinging poison, these creatures inevitably resemble the face of one of the three Gorgons of Greek mythology, namely Medusa, who had snakes for hair and whose gaze would petrify you.

Today, some food is caught in several of the jellyfish's forty-four tentacles, which means Medusa's hair is a little tangled and unkempt.

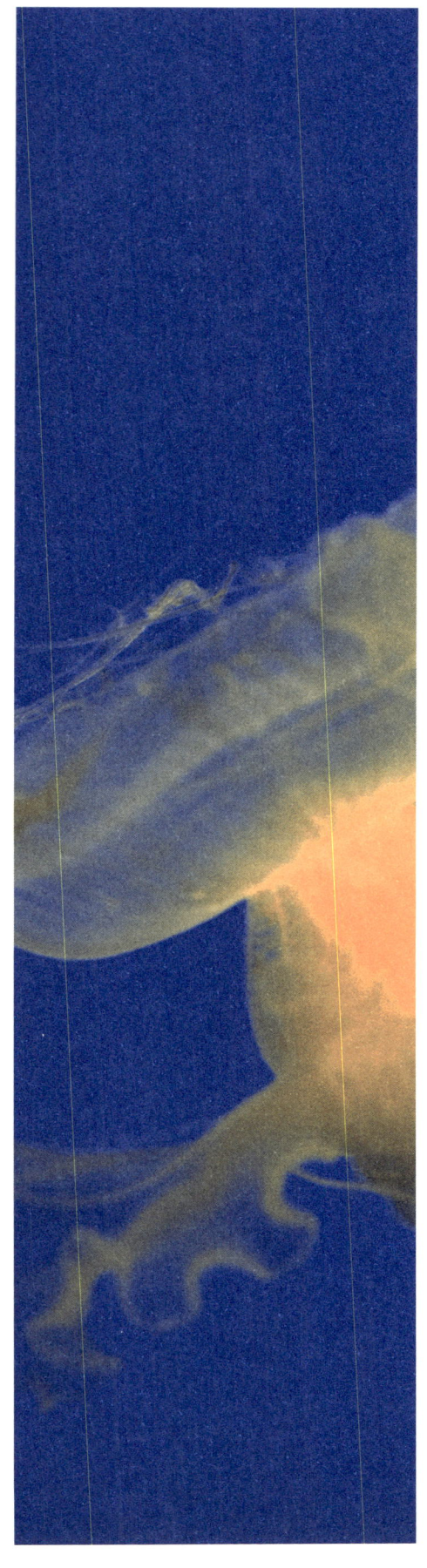

Carl Linnaeus, the Swedish naturalist who gave them a name in the mid eighteenth century, listed these creatures among the zoophytes, that is to say, animal-plants, a separate category for things that couldn't be classified.

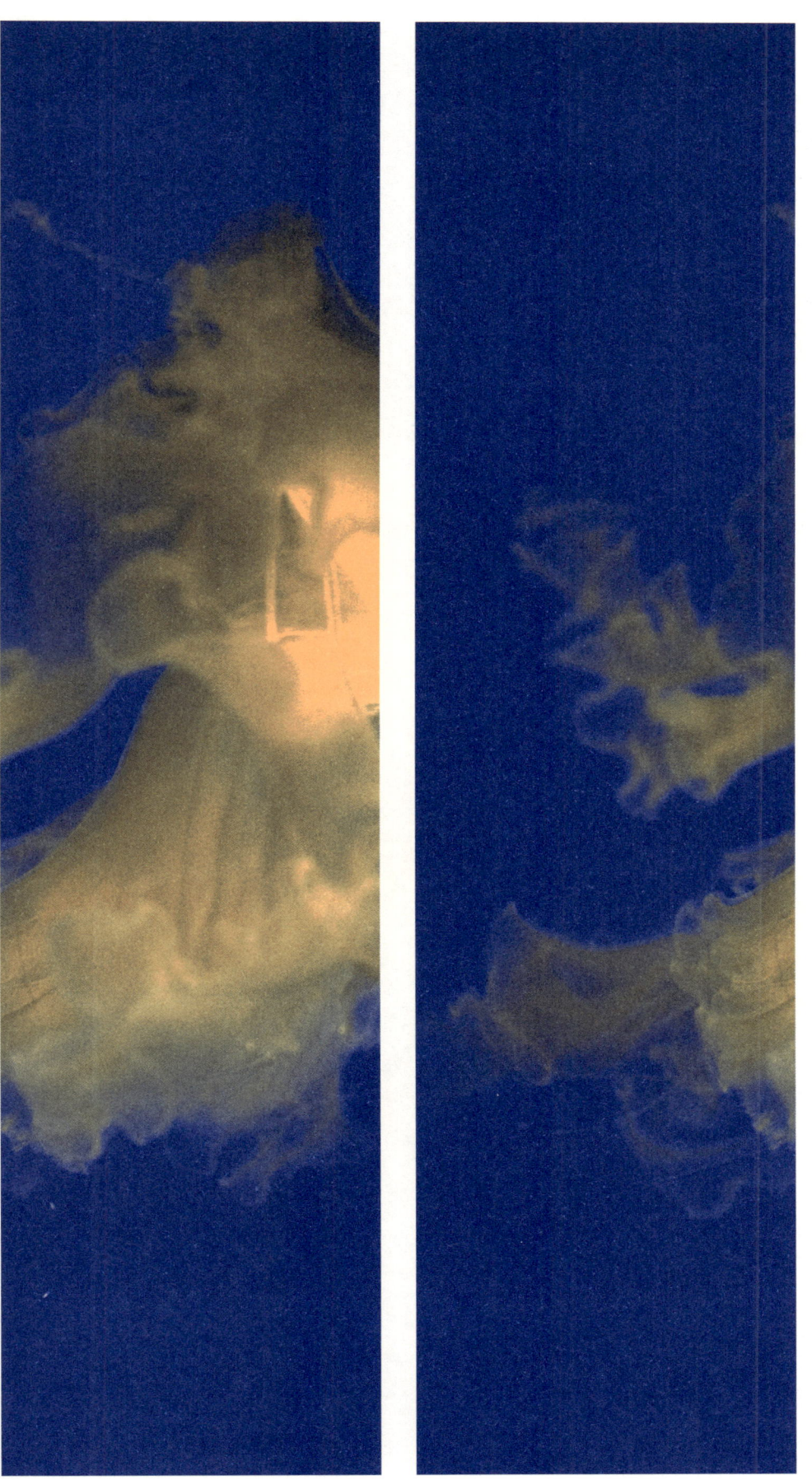

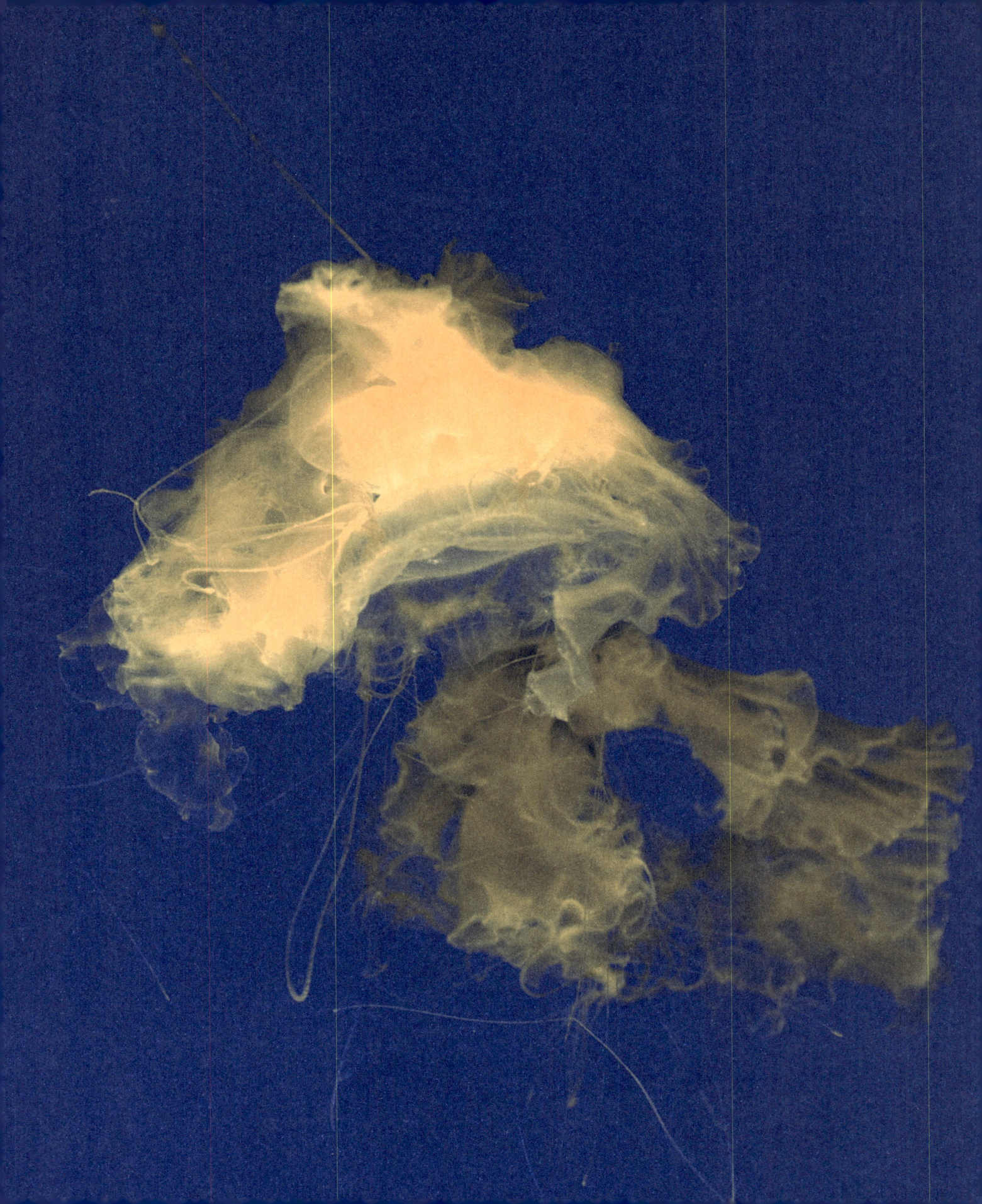

In very ancient times, people said it
used to be a fish just like any other,
with a skeleton, fins and tail.

Then it saved the life of a monkey
whose liver was going to be used to
cure a dying queen.

The king was so furious that he beat
it to a pulp, until it was just a spineless
blob of jelly, the way it is today.

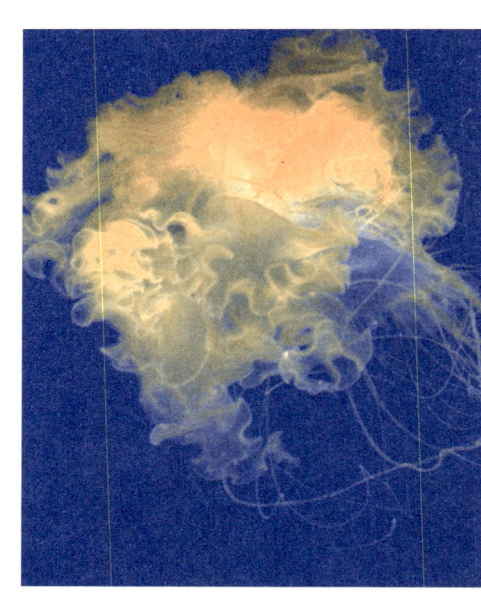
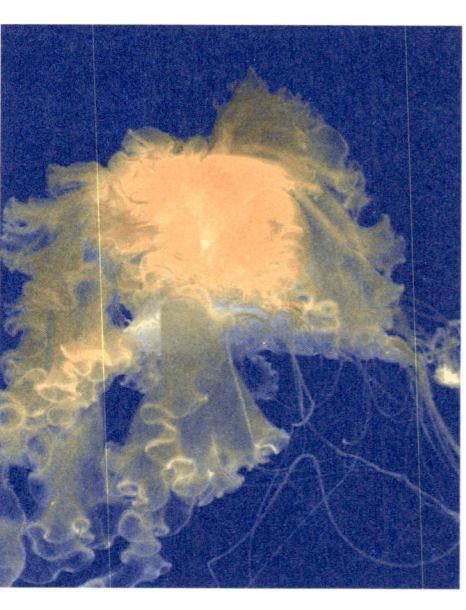

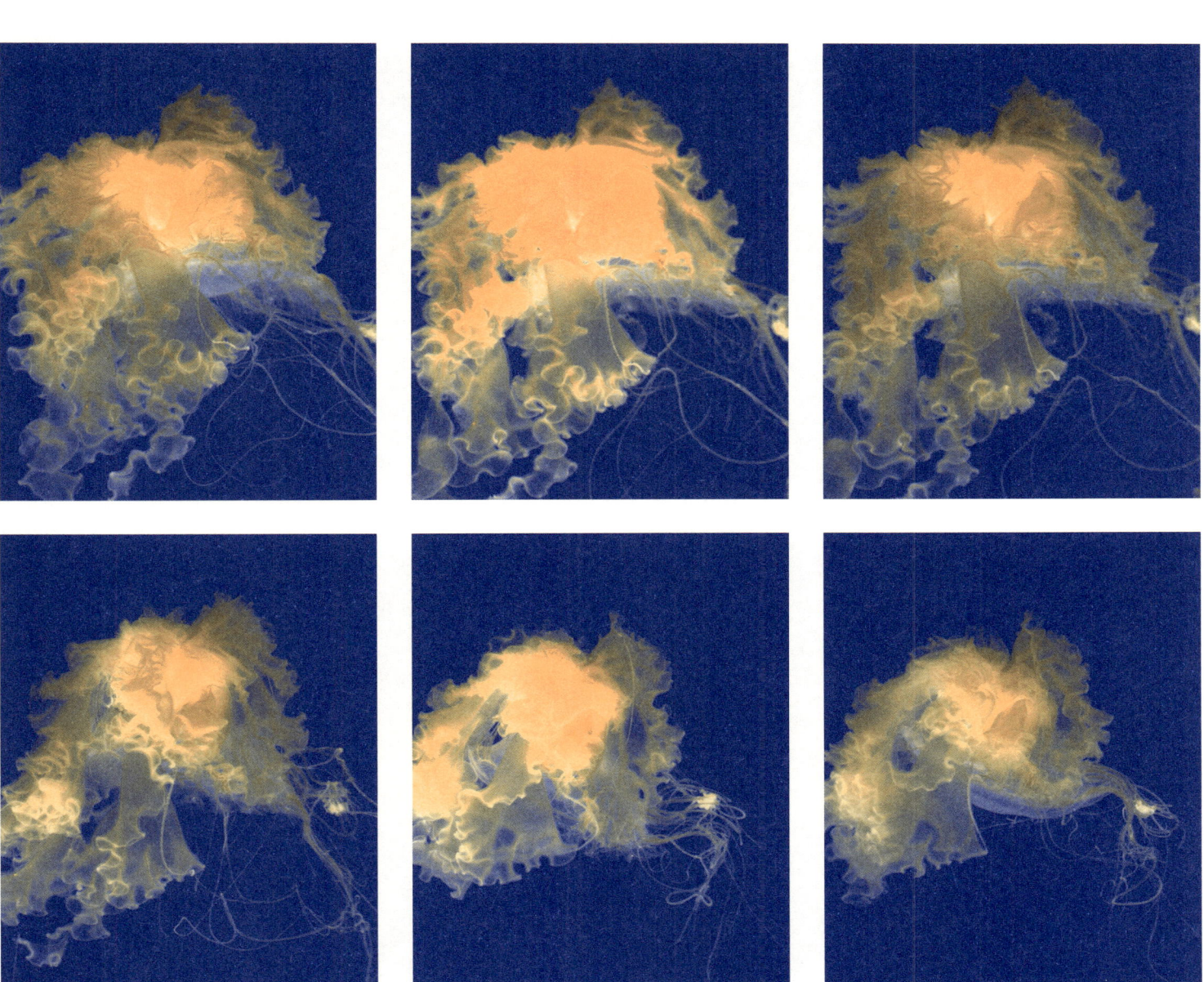

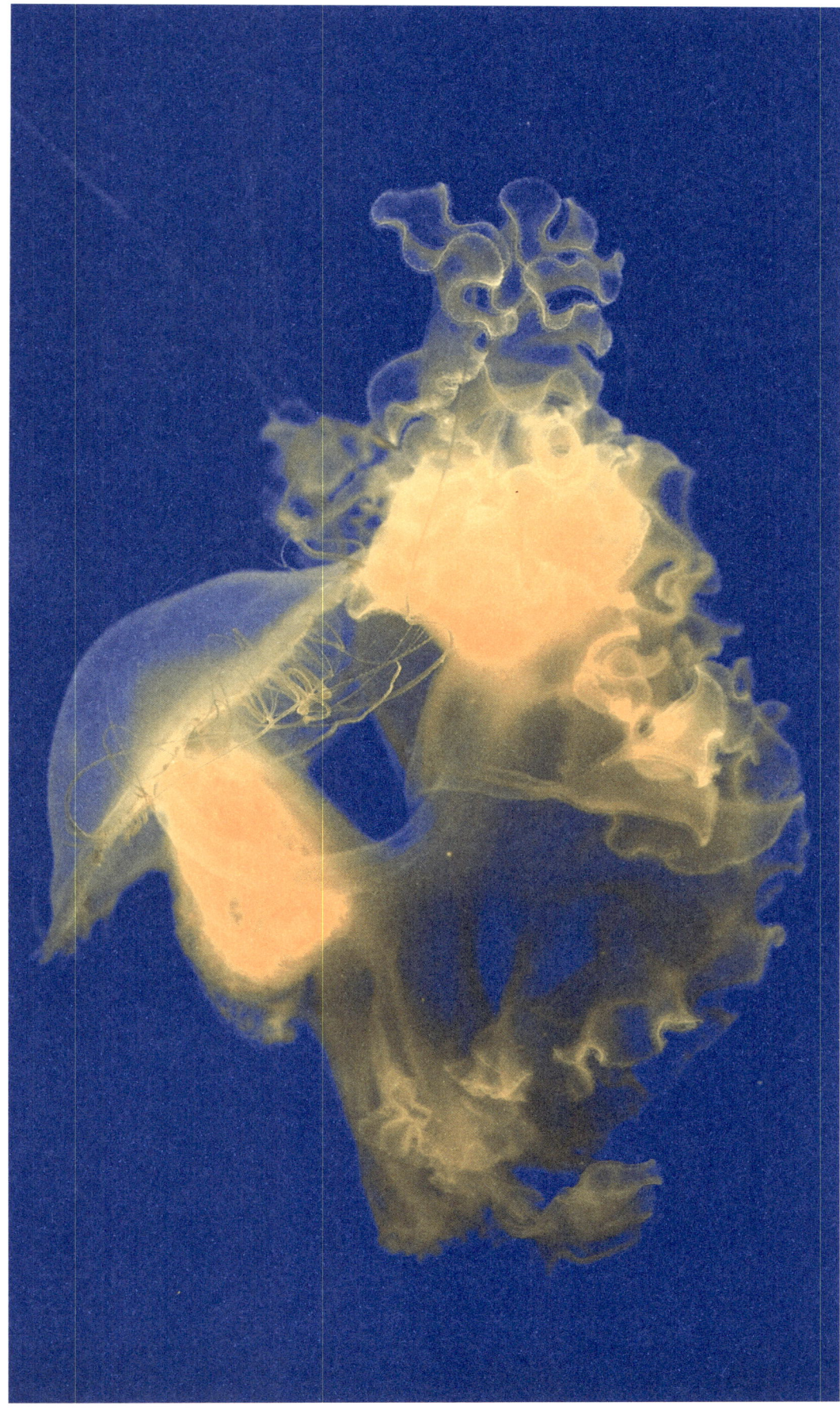

Nothing to distinguish
front from back:
jellyfish just don't fit
the categories.

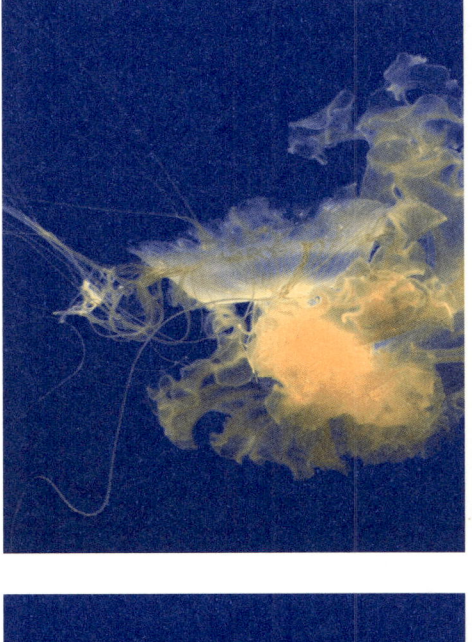 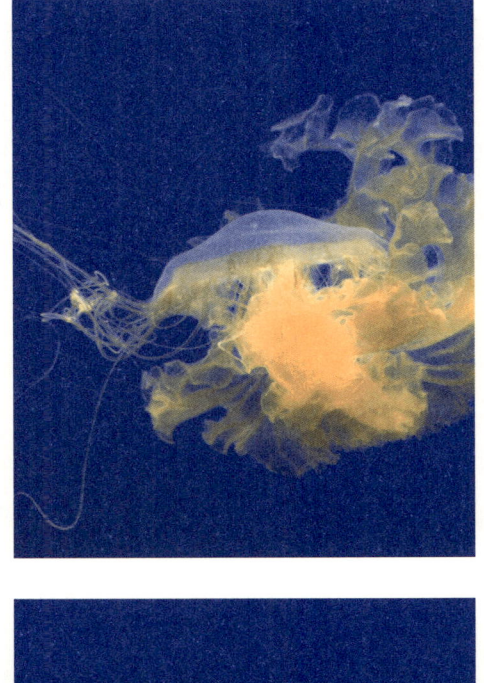 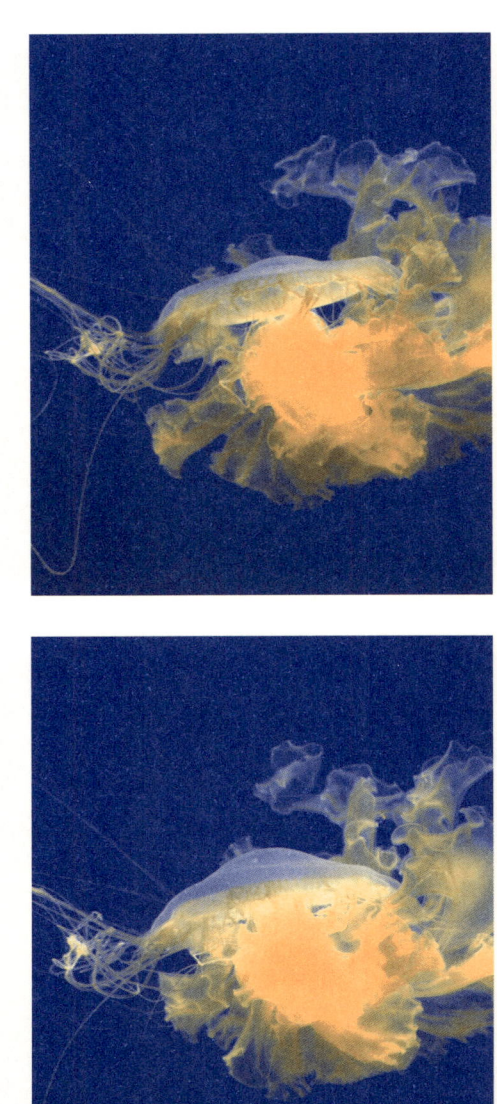

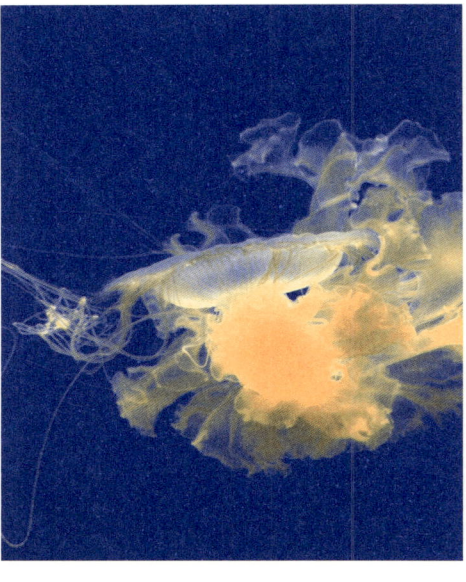 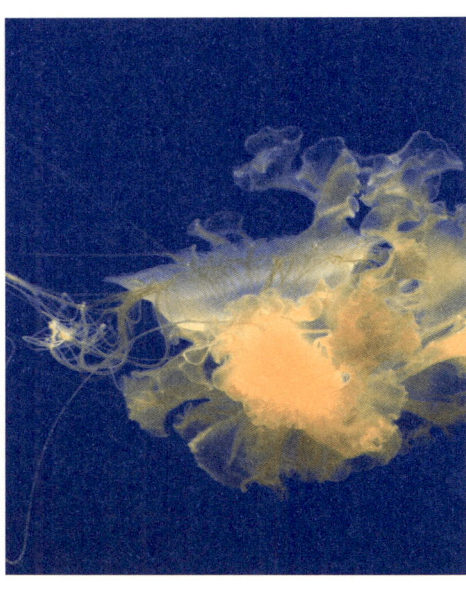 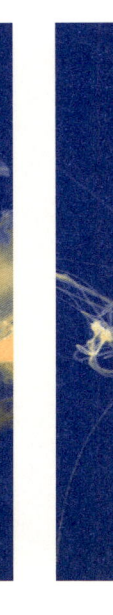

No head

No brain

No bones

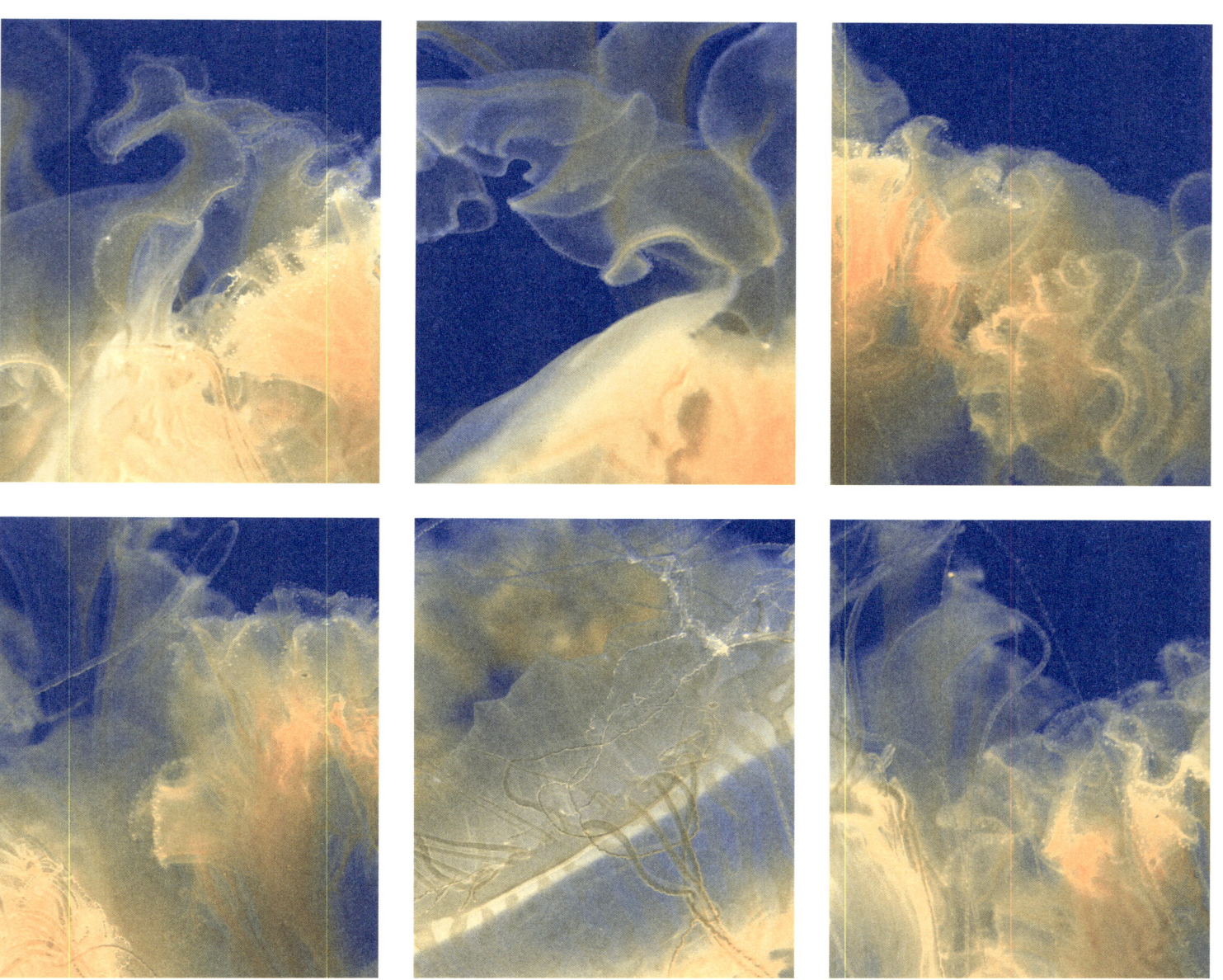

As a powerful hydrating agent, it enhances the elasticity of the skin.

Mesoglea, the gelatinous substance that makes up most of their bodies, contains water in which there abound micro fibrils of collagen.

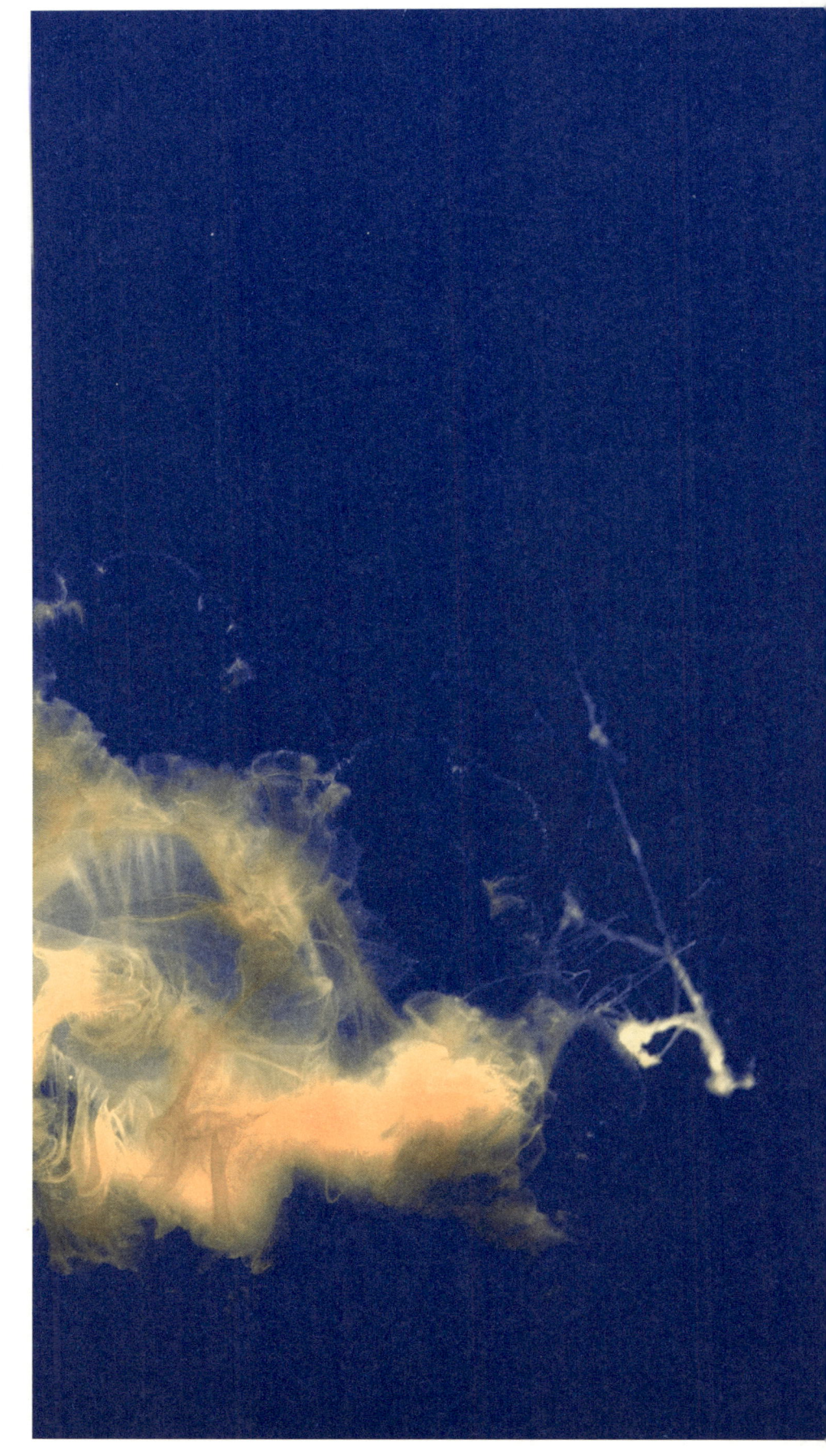

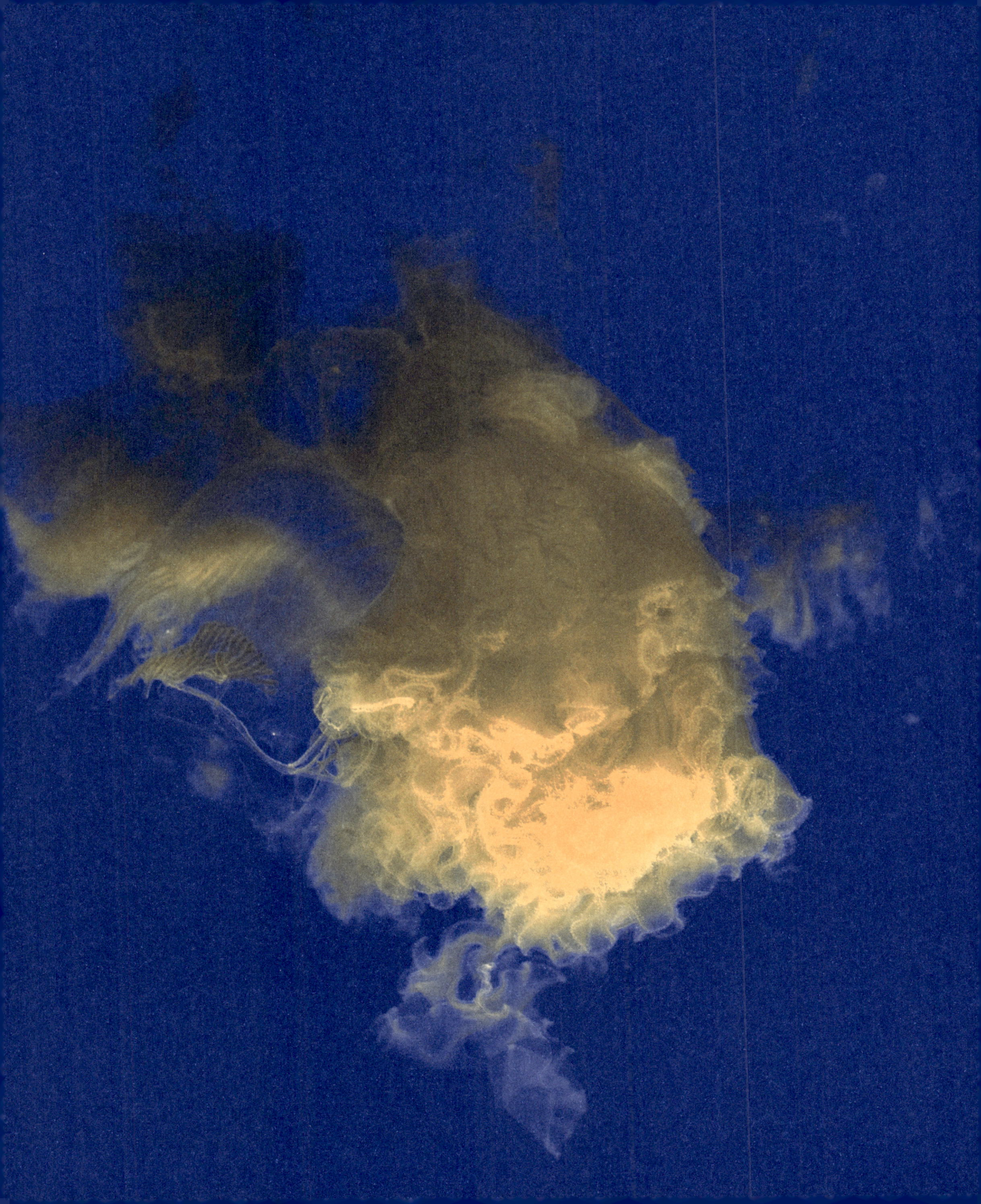

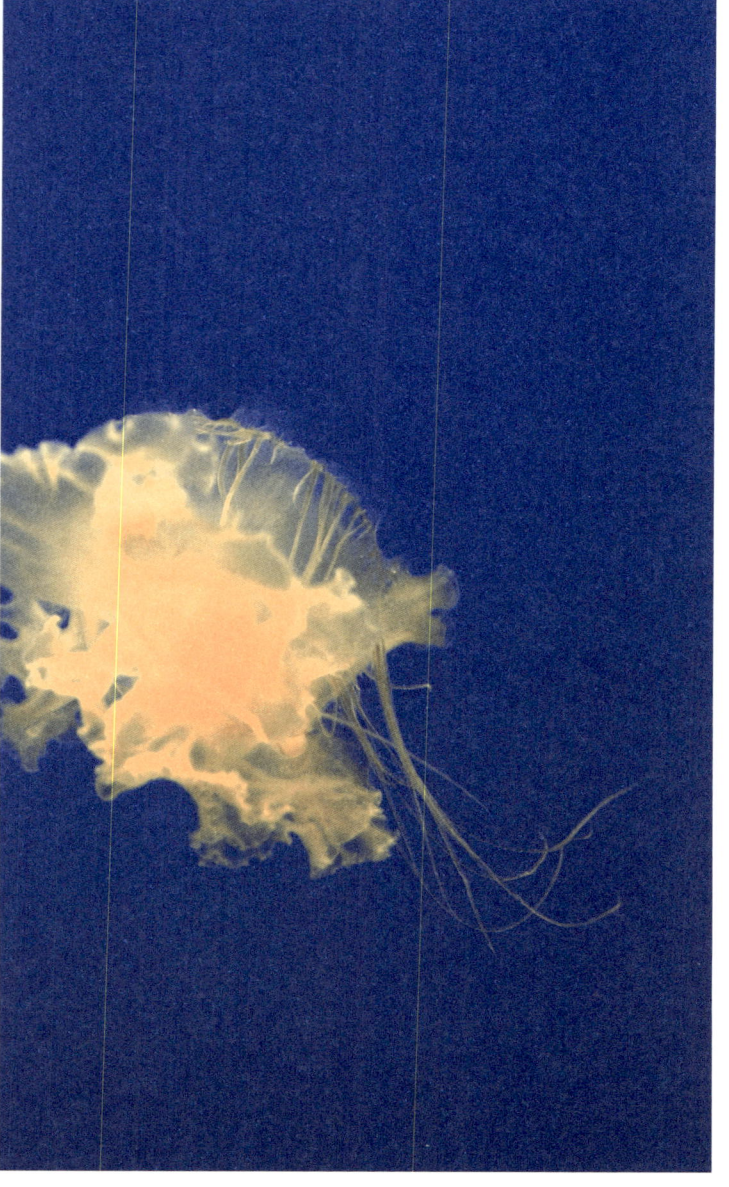

Perfect motion

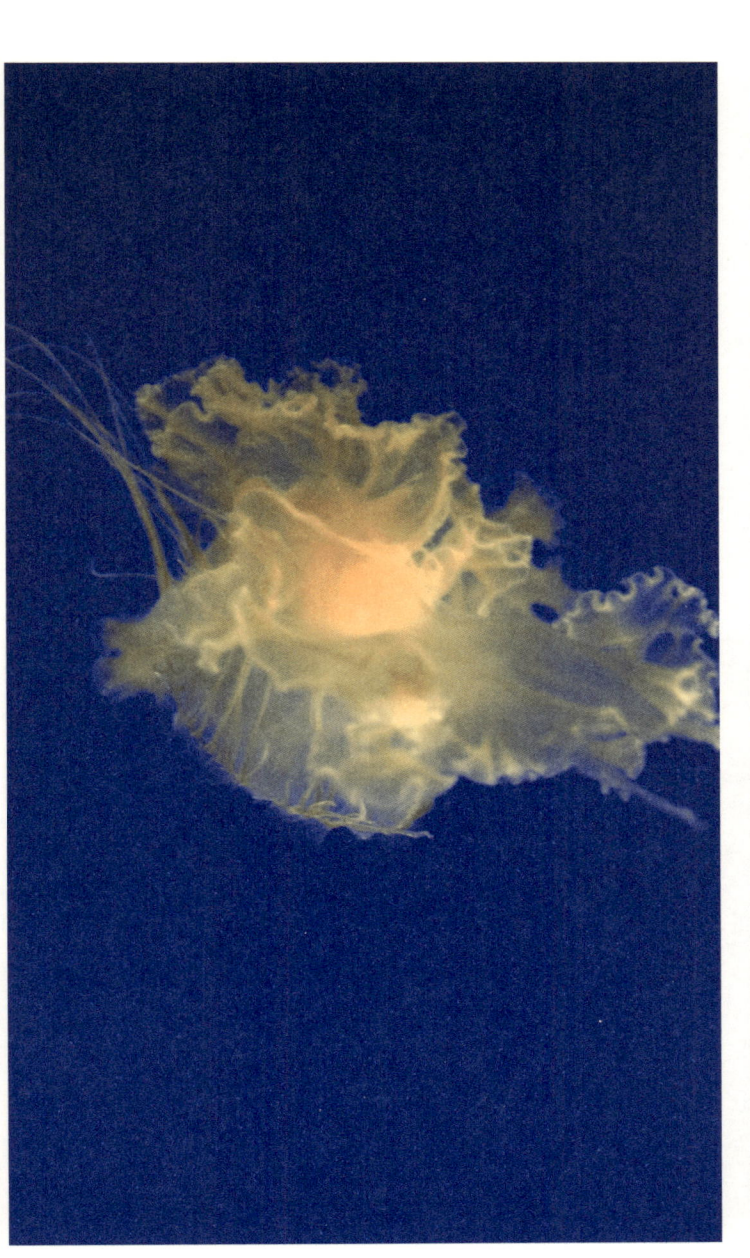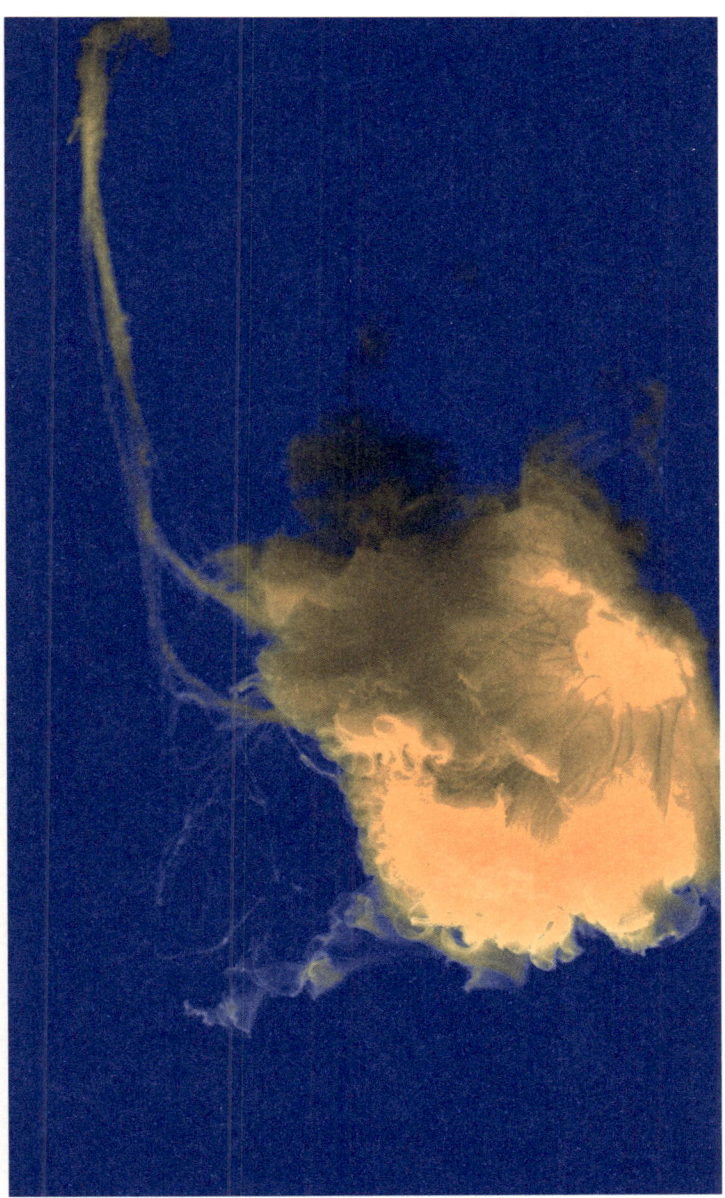

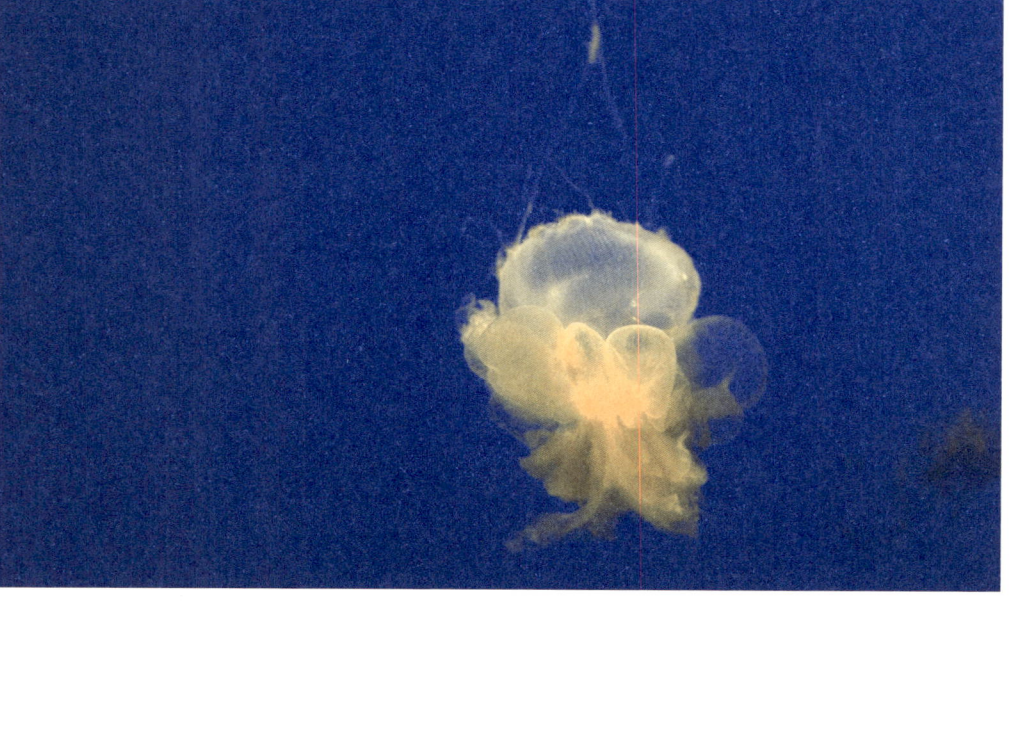

Perfect colours

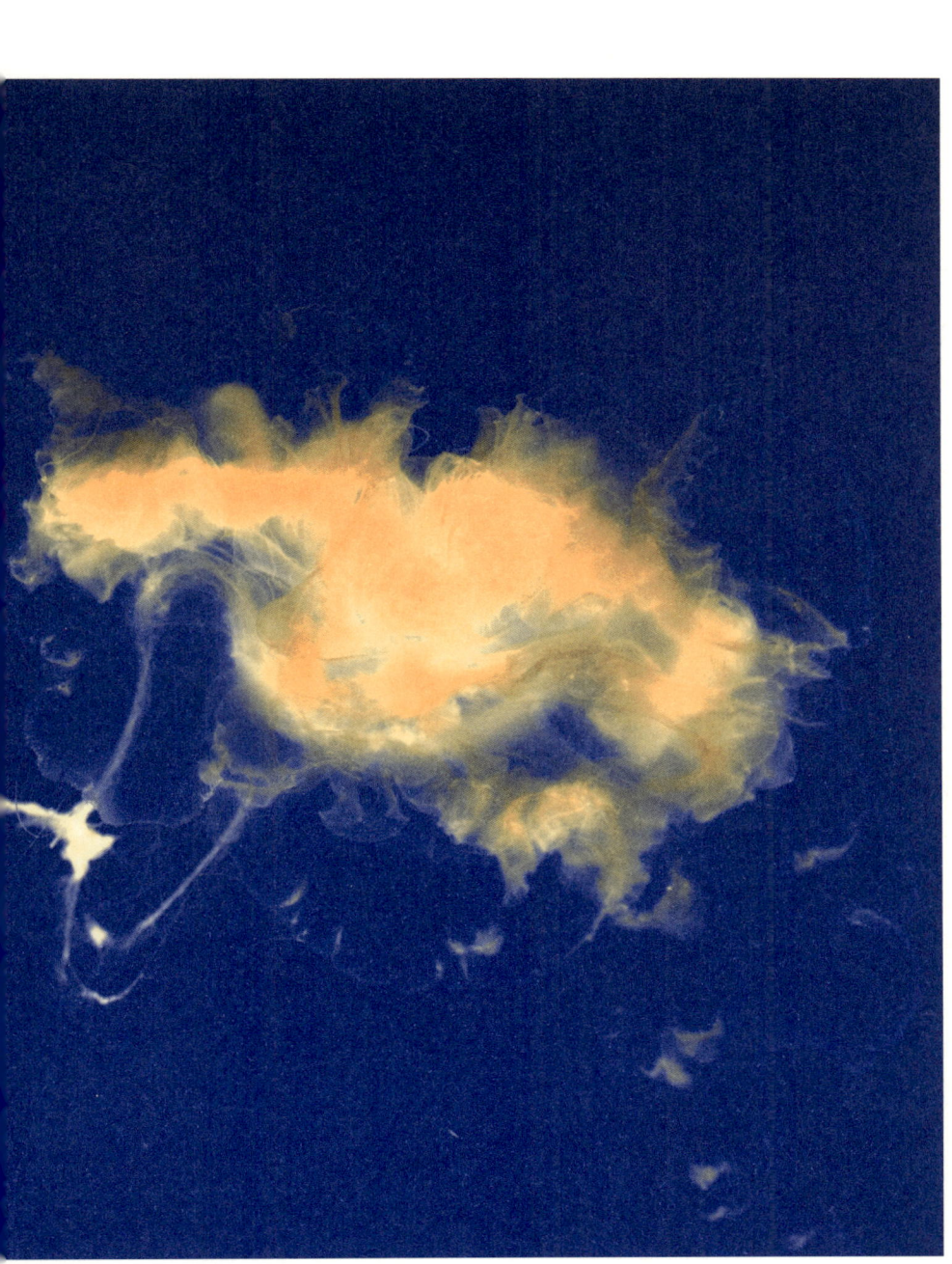

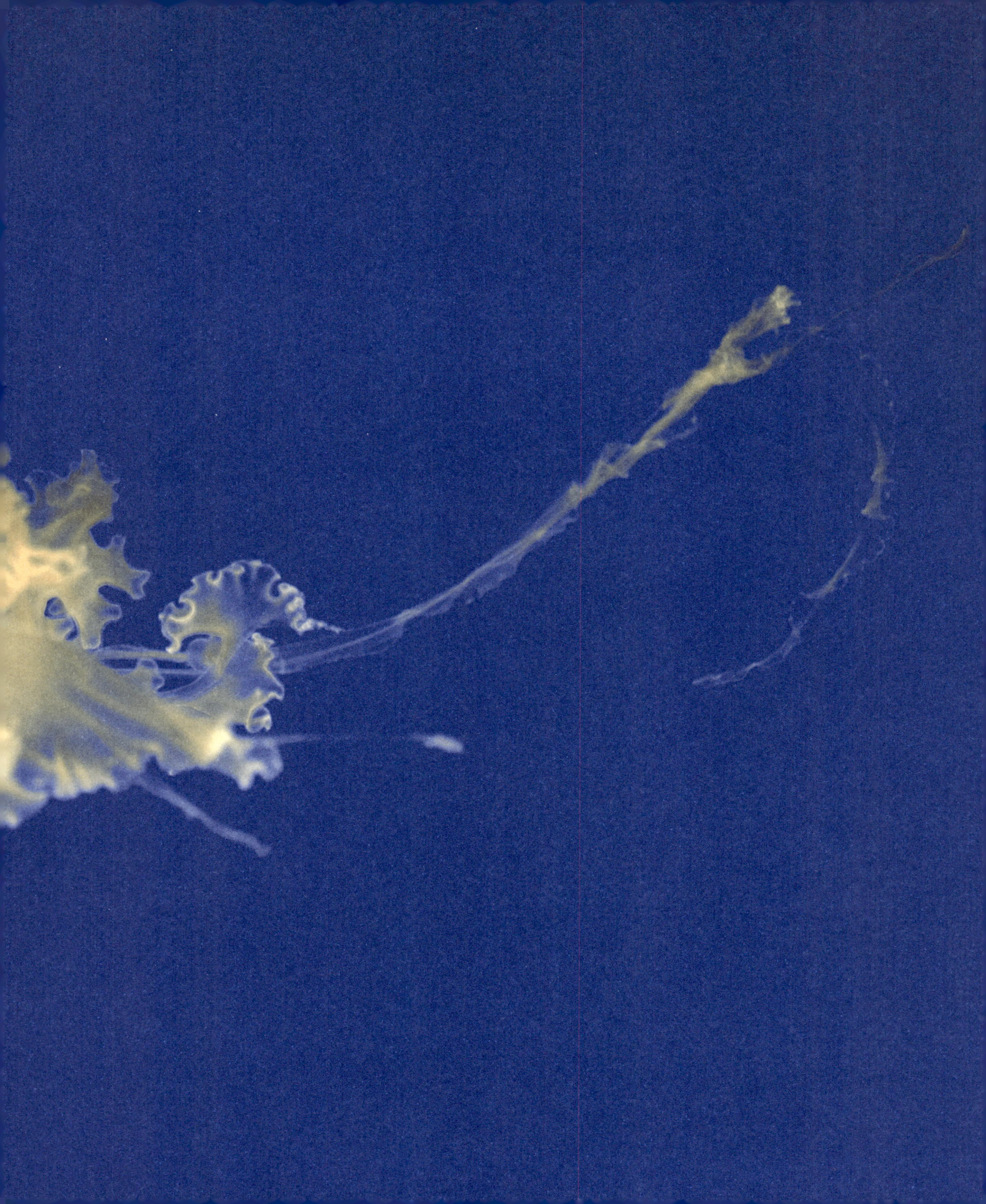

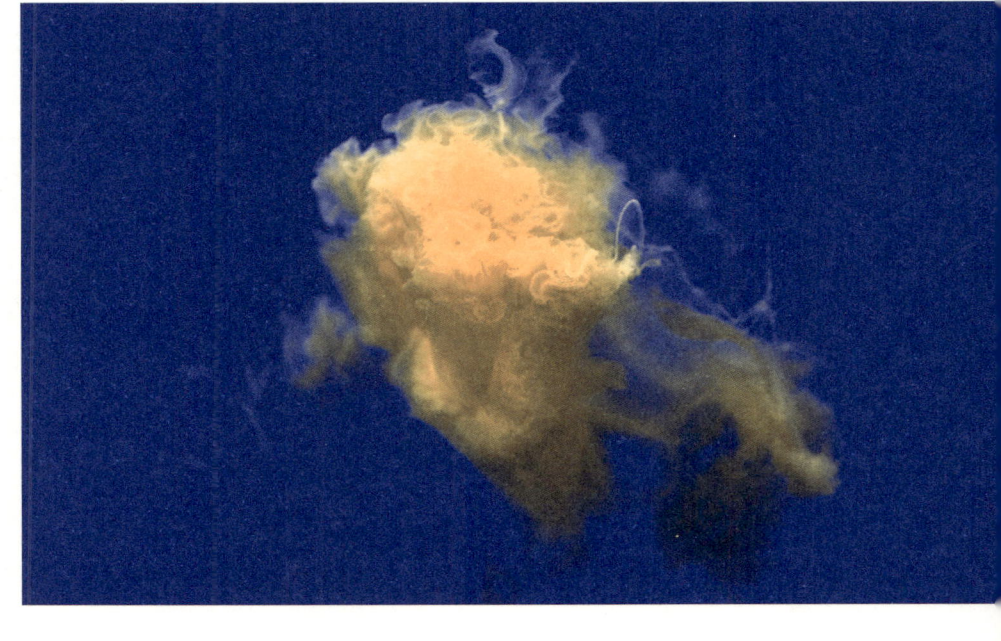

Perfect contrast